THOUGHTS FOR THE TIMES
ON GROUPS AND MASSES
A SIGMUND FREUD MUSEUM SYMPOSIUM

FIGURES OF THE UNCONSCIOUS 22

THOUGHTS FOR THE TIMES ON GROUPS AND MASSES

A Sigmund Freud Museum Symposium

Edited by

Daniela Finzi and Jeanne Wolff Bernstein

LEUVEN UNIVERSITY PRESS

Published with support of Sigmund Freud Foundation Vienna and the Vienna Municipal Department of Cultural Affairs

Sigm. Freud
MUSEUM

Stadt
Wien | Kultur

This book will be made open access under a CC-BY-NC-ND Licence within three years of publication thanks to Path to Open, a program developed in partnership between JSTOR, the American Council of Learned Societies (ACLS), University of Michigan Press, and The University of North Carolina Press to bring about equitable access and impact for the entire scholarly community, including authors, researchers, libraries, and university presses around the world. Learn more at https://about.jstor.org/path-to-open/

As of 2028, attribution to this book should include the CC-licence and read as follows: Daniela Finzi and Jeanne Wolff Bernstein (eds), *Thoughts for the Times on Groups and Masses: A Sigmund Freud Museum Symposium*, Leuven: Leuven University Press, 2028. (CC BY-NC-ND 4.0)

ISBN 978 94 6270 445 9 (paperback)
eISBN 978 94 6166 610 9 (ePDF)
eISBN 978 94 6166 611 6 (ePUB)
https://doi.org/10.11116/9789461666109
D/2025/1869/1
NUR: 770

Typesetting: Friedemann Vervoort
Cover design: Daniel Benneworth-Gray
Cover image: The Protest, 1893, Félix Vallotton, (Swiss French, 1865–1925), France, 19th century. https://www.clevelandart.org/art/1999.323

GPRC
Guaranteed
Peer Reviewed
Content
www.gprc.be

Dedicated to
Professor Sophie Freud

Contents

Preface

International experts from the fields of psychoanalysis, psychiatry, psychology, sociology, philosophy, and linguistics and literature came together at the conference *Thoughts for the Times on Groups and Masses* organized by the Freud Museum in June 2022 in order to analyze current group and mass phenomena that shape the image of our societies. Following our leitmotif SPEAKING FREELY, we focused on psycho-social issues in the context of continuing refugee movements and, more than ever, the theatres of war that are erupting across the globe. Among others, the conference considered issues like identity conflicts and aspirations to autonomy, increasing tendencies towards paranoia and denial, and aggressions based on religious, racist, sexist, and homophobic motives.

Freud already referred to the correlating relationship between the individual and the collective psyche in his 1921 text *Group Psychology and the Analysis of the Ego,* suggesting that the difference between individual and social psychology only seemed meaningful at first glance, as "someone else is invariably involved, as a model, as an object, as a helper, as an opponent; and so from the very first individual psychology […] is at the same time social psychology as well."[1]

All her life, professor Sophie Freud, Sigmund Freud's granddaughter and a dear friend of Berggasse 19, also addressed the mutual conditionality of psychological and social dimensions in her work as a psychologist and social scientist. As a victim of the Shoah, the biggest movement of persecution and extermination of the 20th century, she also confronted her personal traumatizing experiences in her literary works. Sophie Freud died on June 3, 2022 in the US, aged 97 – in remembrance to her open, always alert and critical character, the conference as well as the corresponding publication were dedicated to her.

I would like to thank Jeanne Wolff-Bernstein, the chair of our scientific advisory board, as well as Daniela Finzi, our research director, for the conception and organization of this important conference. Our special thanks go to the speakers, whose theoretical and praxis-oriented contributions we can now present in this volume, offering valuable insights into the multi-layered subject of current group and mass phenomena, but also highlighting positive tendencies of future developments.

Monika Pessler
Director
Sigmund Freud Museum, Vienna

Notes

[1] Sigmund Freud, *Group Psychology and the Analysis of the Ego* (1921), *SE 18*, pp. 65-143, p. 69.

Introduction

Daniela Finzi and Jeanne Wolff Bernstein

This collection of essays selected for the symposium 'Thoughts for the Times on Groups and Masses' could not have appeared at a more poignant time in history than the present. Initially planned to commemorate the 100th anniversary of Freud's 1921 canonical text *Group Psychology and the Analysis of the Ego*, the symposium at Berggasse 19 in Vienna was postponed for a year due to the constrictions of the Covid pandemic. Now, after a hiatus of almost two years, the significance of these texts has gained exponentially in importance, given the current turmoil around the globe. As a matter of fact, today we live in a world characterized by a multitude of overlapping crises: climate change and the pandemic, forced migration, terrorism, wars, and the rise of authoritarian structures combine with a massive media transformation, a digital modification of the structures of public space, and an alarming decline of democratic values as well as the demise of certainties long held to be self-evident.

It really does not take a lot of imagination to draw parallels with the period a good 100 years ago when Sigmund Freud published *Group Psychology and the Analysis of the Ego* in the summer of 1921. Alongside *The Future of an Illusion*, *Civilization and Its Discontents* and *Moses and Monotheism*, this work belongs to the ensemble of cultural theory texts, the third group of his writings alongside the pre-analytical ones from the 1880s and 1890s and the psychological writings from the first two decades of the 20th century.[1] Freud's initial ideas for this text focusing on social and mass psychology date back to the spring of 1919 – a time marked by the end of the First World War and the proclamation of the First Austrian Republic. Political upheavals and economic hardship led to unrest among the population and numerous mass strikes, which prompted Freud and his colleagues to take a closer look at social reality. The focus of the Fifth International Psychoanalytic Congress in Budapest, September 28-29, 1918, was 'The Psycho-Analysis of War Neuroses';[2] in February 1919, Victor Tausk gave a lecture on 'War Neuroses and War Psychoses' at the meeting of the Vienna Psychoanalytic Society (Wiener Psychoanalytische Vereinigung,

WPV), and a few weeks later, on March 23, Paul Federn, one of Freud's oldest and most loyal colleagues and an active socialist, was discussing "The fatherless society",[3] which also resulted in a little brochure.[4] According to Ernst Federn, his son, this publication was not only the first real application of psychoanalysis to political issues,[5] but it also directly motivated Freud to formulate his views on mass psychology, or – as Sándor Ferenczi had put it succinctly – to tackle a "dissection of the mass soul"[6].

Taking recourse to his earlier texts *Totem and Taboo* (1912) and *On Narcissism: An Introduction* (1914), Freud describes the erotic cathexes underlying the idealization of a strong father figure, which simultaneously results in an identification with the lost inner ego ideal. In contrast to the descriptive, more controversial works of his predecessors, Gustave Le Bon (*The Crowd. A Study of the Popular Mind,* 1895) and William McDougall (*The Group Mind,* 1920), Freud's *Group Psychology and the Analysis of the Ego* is characterized by an analytic scrutiny of the transformation of the individual to a group being: what defines the "group", what keeps it together, what kind of satisfaction – the "crooked cures"[7] ("Schiefheilungen") – is an emergence into the group able to provide, what unconscious mechanisms and psychological phenomena are at work when a multitude of individuals submit to a "leader" – these are key questions that we can gather from the text.

Although this text – which has also accompanied the careers of numerous sociologists, social psychologists, and group analysts – was to remain the only work of Freud which can be attributed to sociology in the broadest sense, the commonly held idea, also shared by psychoanalysts themselves, that psychoanalysis only views the individual as a monad, beleaguered by internal conflicts, is neither correct nor can it be seriously upheld in this day and age. While other fields of study were traditionally deemed to be *applied,* the hegemony of psychoanalysis believed itself to be a secure, distinct, and instructive discipline for others. However, once it became evident that the separation of inner and outer was not so easily drawn, and that the *social* and the *individual* were intricately interwoven and basically inseparable, the critique of studies devoted to fathoming societal problems became increasingly exacting and convoluted.

Ultimately, it was Sigmund Freud himself who paved the way for the notion that the human being is primarily a social creature and not an isolated being unaffected by the external world. "From the first individual psychology in this extended but entirely justifiable sense of words", he wrote, "is at the same time social psychology as well."[8] "The mind is a palimpsest in which the traces of these figures will jostle and rearrange themselves for everyone. [...]

Our 'psyche' is a social space",[9] Jacqueline Rose also writes in her introduction to the 2004 penguin edition of *Mass Psychology and Other Writings*, which is well worth reading. The translator is JA Underwood, who renders the German term "Masse" as "mass" – and thus makes a striking change to the title of the Standard Edition. In fact, the first translation of Freud's work into English – under the title *Group Psychology and the Analysis of the Ego*[10] – by James Strachey had already been published by the International Psycho-Analytical Press the following year, in 1922: When Freud was working on the text, the word "group" was still relatively rarely in use in German,[11] and of course groups also often exhibit the structure of Freud's regressive mass bonding. For this reason, the title of this anthology also contains both terms, group and mass – which admittedly opens up different horizons of association, which also applies to the contributions of this volume.

In the first article, 'Sexual Drives, Eros, and Identification – A Re-reading of Freud's *Group Psychology and the Analysis of the Ego*', Ulrike May methodically reconstructs the genesis of Freud's writing. Her text reads like a detective story and uncovers evidence against James Strachey's authoritative argument that "there is little direct connection between the present work and its close predecessor, *Beyond the Pleasure Principle*",[12] revealing that there are intricate connections between the two and that a close "temporal proximity" exists between the two texts. Notably, May remarks that many of Freud's most radical ideas typically appear in the seventh chapter of his *oeuvre*, subsequently providing a concise summary of the difference between identification and libidinal object cathexis: "in the case of identification, the object is what one *wants to be*; in the case of libidinal object relations, the object is what one *wants to have*."[13]

It is striking that Freud, without even providing any description of the leader figure(s) on which his undertaking is based, draws on examples from the political sphere that formed the central pillars of the monarchy which had just come to an end. However, he omits the movements of the period of upheaval in which he found himself, characterized by revolutions, large mass strikes and mass movements, as well as anti-Semitism – only in the years following the publication of the book would he increasingly take a position on this.[14] Nevertheless, there is an implicit political dimension inherent in Freud's *Group Psychology*. It is important to bear in mind that the National Socialist movement began its triumphal march in the very years following its publication. The nature of this leader-centered mass – after all, Hitler allowed himself to be called simply "The Führer" – corresponded so obviously with

Freud's explanations that Theodor W. Adorno would later, in 1951, base his own analysis of the social psychology of National Socialism very directly on them.[15] Adorno was convinced that Freud, although he was hardly interested in the political side of the problem, clearly foresaw the emergence and nature of fascist mass movements in purely psychological categories. It is by the next contributor, Helmut Dahmer, who focuses in his chapter 'Freud's "Mass Psychology"' on the historical relationship between the masses and the individual, that the sociological perspective is introduced. In dialog with the canonical authors of sociology, he is also interested in the links to today's masses, including contemporary forms of mass communication.

The fact that we are standing at a crossroad of turbulent and troubling times applies not only to world statecraft but also to the politics of the psychoanalytic movement. The question of what is truly psychoanalytic or what is just a watered-down psychoanalytic study of societal conflicts has reemerged with voices from near and far, from young and old who believe that psychoanalysis has drifted too far away from its initial focus on the intra-psychic unconscious dynamics of the individual. Concerned by an increased interest in the psychoanalytic examination of rightwing and populist movements and leaders, conspiracy theories, the impact of technology and climate change upon humanity, many practitioners in the psychoanalytic movement fear that psychoanalysts place too much emphasis on the external world, and are thereby not paying sufficient heed to the subject's inner, repressed unconscious fantasies to the morass of outside events. The texts of Earl Hopper and Francisco González offer a welcome corrective to this traditional trend of thinking, momentarily extricating the individual from society at large. Both papers convincingly argue for the idea that the analysand is an "inter-subject" and cannot be detached from their social history and context. Hopper starts from the assumption that trauma and helplessness are at the core of the human condition. In his article 'The Social Unconscious, Trauma and Groups: A Constellation' he presents his understanding of the concept of the "social unconscious" as well as his theory of the forth basic assumption – "Incohesion: Aggregation/Massification" –, which is a group-analytical further development of Wilfred R. Bion's theory of the three basic assumptions (dependency, fight-flight, and pairing), in order to shift the focus to the process of the loss of bonding structures and cohesion in social systems. Francisco J. González also refers to the concept of the social unconscious and to group-analytical insights in his contribution 'The In-Between of Us: The Inter-Subject and Interstitial Belonging' in order to explore what constitutes "belonging". González starts from the idea of a double origin of the unconscious to problematize collective aspects of individual subjectivity and the subjective aspects of collective ensembles. His contribution concludes with a vow to his psychoanalytic colleagues to no longer exclude the dimension of the social unconscious, but to enable a "trans-mural" psychoanalysis, as it were. Criticism of the failure of psychoanalysis as an institution to deal with important political issues also resonates in Ranjana Khanna's contribution 'Mass Death / Tobacco and Salt'. After all, she discusses Jacques Derrida's opening address 'Geopsychoanalysis: "... and the rest of the world"' to a French-Latin American meeting convened in Paris in 1981 before turning to Freud's 'Thoughts for the Times on War and Death' (1915) in order to discuss the question of individual agency in relation to mass death.

Another focus of the conference was the examination of mass psychology in virtual space, as today it is the Internet that is able to mobilize the masses like no other medium. At the same time, as Sama Maani points out in 'Art, Identity, and Group Psychology in Digital Modernity', the concept of mass formation seems misleading in that the virtual mass constituted via the Internet consists of highly isolated, atomized individuals. Also, the members of the masses, he rightly points out, no longer want to be part of a group, they want to be unique:

> This is what has been voiced and promoted for decades now by the narcissistic *imperatives of authenticity* that are omnipresent in advertising, in the culture industry, in pop-psych self-help literature, etc., by saying 'Be yourself,' 'Believe in yourself,' 'Achieve your best self'.[16]

It is interesting to note how these two currents manage to coexist side by side: an intense surrender and devotion to a corrupt and perverse Other in the form of various malignant narcissistic leaders ("*Führer*") across the world, and a markedly amplified withdrawal into a narcissistic cocoon that preserves an intense involvement and preoccupation with oneself. Jan de Vos' article 'The Truths of Psychoanalysis: Defying the Lies of Psychology that Fuel the Digital Amassing of Individuals' is also based on the massive media transformation and digital restructuring of the public sphere, which enables the "algorithmic amassing of people". De Vos is interested in the capacity of psychoanalysis not only to understand the dynamics of digital appropriation, but also the ways in which it can contribute to resisting them. Giuseppina Antinucci, in turn combines theoretical and clinical insights in her contribution 'Representing the Crisis of Representation', illustrating how early this narcissistic investment in one's own self may begin in our current technology-driven culture, in which the omnipresence of electronic devices occupies or contaminates the space of imagination and thought, and thus makes it possible, as it were, to circumvent a central component of becoming a subject – namely renunciation. Given the disembodied early universe with its faceless individualities, it is perhaps no surprise that millions of people swarm once again towards leaders who seemingly provide them with a much longed-for, albeit porous, sense of identity.

The final two chapters take an in-depth look at the storming of the Capitol on January 6, 2021 by supporters of then still incumbent but already voted out US President Donald Trump. Drawing on Freud's *Group Psychology*, on Vamik Vulkan's works and Otto Kernberg's insights on narcissism, Ricardo Ainslie in 'Ideology, Leaders, and Group Actions in the January 6 Insurrection' draws upon the violent events to shed light on the processes of regression and disinhibition that can be at work in groups. Also, Ainslie distinguishes between three different groups of supporters who came together. Gail Newman, on the other hand, draws attention to the differences and limitations of Freud's writing in her article '*Massenpsychologie* and MAGA': She points out that what constituted a basic premise of Freud's text and time – namely, the presence of "Thirdness", a triangulating agency that enables the shared understanding of a moral and epistemological reality – has been eroded and collapsed into binarism in neoliberal thought. According to Newman who underscores the crucial difference Freud draws between object cathexis and identification, one that May had already pointed out in her previous text, Trump's MAGA following does not so much desire what he *has* as what he *is*: Skirting the Third, the masses and mobs cheering Trump yearn to merge with him, a perfect idol of oneness that does not encourage any differentiation or separation from him but instead promises a nostalgic return to "a lost imaginary past",[17] i.e., an America that was once great but no longer is, a nation that can only become great again through Trump's absolutist vision. Newman's analysis of the Trump phenomenon that so many have been trying to unravel for the last four years perfectly applies to an article recently published in the *Washington Post* on January 11, 2024, a day before the Iowa caucus, analyzing the evening debate between the Republican candidates DeSantis and Haley, a gathering Trump conspicuously avoided, choosing instead to attend a town hall meeting organized by Fox News. While the two contestants were sparring, Trump jovially entertained an audience invited and selected by Fox News. Philip Bump, a national columnist describes the event as follows:

The most revealing moment during Donald Trump's town hall interview that aired on Fox News…wasn't about his past service as president or even his future desire to regain that position. Instead, it came when a woman named Kim stood up to ask Trump a question.

Do you know who you're caucusing for Monday? Fox News's Bret Baier asked.

I am proud to say I am a caucus captain! Kim replied.

For? Baier prompted.

President Trump! Kim replied, pointing at the former president.

With a white-and-gold hat, Trump interjected.

I have that white-and-gold hat, Kim replied.

That's it, in a nutshell. Trump is famous and powerful and viewed by many Americans as the country's salvation. He is also the guy who spent decades tailoring his ability to get people to buy stuff with the word "Trump" on it, figuring out how to build loyalty to his brand both with gimmicks and by cultivating the sense that customers were entering his world of luxury.

So that goofy hat wasn't just a hat. It was a symbol that Kim was part of Trump's essential inner circle. Kim and her fellow caucus captains are, for the next week or so, some of the most important people in Trump's world, and that hat proves it.[18]

Of the many stories and anecdotes published about Donald Trump, this story illustrates in utter simplicity the mechanism Trumps employs – among many others – to titillate and lure his adult audiences into a kind of simple-minded, gigantic infantile birthday-party-like gathering, during which audiences are drawn into a make-believe world, à la Mr. Rogers,[19] fulfilling their unconscious desires to equate with their idol and participate in this glittering gold and blue jamboree. In light of this illusion, the much-quoted sentence from Freud's *Group Psychology and the Analysis of the Ego* proves to be prescient in understanding this dynamic: "In groups the most contradictory ideas can exist side by side and tolerate each other, without any conflict arising from the logical contradiction between them."[20] In this hypnotic "mob" type of setting that has become a Trump staple, his admirers seem to forget completely that he was the one destroying the very social universe from which he now claims to rescue them without any detailed explanations.

Daniela Finzi and Jeanne Wolff Bernstein

We think this volume of essays honoring Freud's *Group Psychology and the Analysis of the Ego* on its 100th anniversary illustrates what T.S. Eliot once termed, "how to work the dead". Contrasting the idea that there is no linearity of time, Eliot wrote in *The Tradition and the Individual Talent,* that

> no poet, no artist [and here we might add, no psychoanalyst] has his complete meaning alone. His significance, his appreciation is the relation to the dead poets and artists [again, psychoanalysts included]. You cannot value him alone, but must set him, for contrasts and comparisons, among the dead.[21]

The collection of essays assembled in this volume speaks to the evocative nature of Freud's 1921 essay *Group Psychology and the Analysis of the Ego,* which while marking a caesura in his thinking at that time, foreshadowed the lasting significance and usefulness of his theory for analyzing the deeply troubling mass and group phenomena of today's media-driven world.

This volume would not have been possible without the support of the Sigmund Freud Foundation Vienna and the Vienna Municipal Department of Cultural Affairs. We would like to thank Sarah Dunkee, Brita Pohl and Bettina Mathes for their translation work, and Andrew Ellis and Johanna Frei for copy-editing.

Notes

1 See H. Dahmer, *Die unnatürliche Wissenschaft. Soziologische Freud-Lektüren.* Münster: Westfälisches Dampfboot, 2012, p. 16.
2 It was also at this first meeting of IPV members since 1913 that Freud called for the creation of psychoanalytic treatment centers for poorer classes – thus providing the decisive impetus for the founding of the Psychoanalytic Polyclinic in Berlin in 1920 and the Vienna Psychoanalytic Polyclinic in 1922.
3 See K. Fallend, *Sonderlinge, Träumer, Sensitive. Psychoanalyse auf dem Weg zur Institution und Profession.* Protokolle der Wiener Psychoanalytischen Vereinigung und biographische Studien, Vienna: Verlag Volk & Welt, 1995, p. 155 a. 168. Fallend discovered the previously unknown minutes of meetings of the WPV from the years 1919 to 1923 in the estate of Siegfried Bernfeld, which is kept in the Library of Congress, Washington D.C.
4 P. Federn, *Die vaterlose Gesellschaft. Zur Psychologie der Revolution. Nach Vorträgen in der Wiener Psychoanalytischen Vereinigung und im Monistenbund.* Vienna: Anzengruber Verlag, 1919.

5   See J. van Ginneken, 'Die Vatertötung. Über die Hintergründe von Freuds "Massen-psychologie und Ich-Analyse"', in: *Psyche* 38 (1984), p. 1124-1148, p. 1134.

6   S. Ferenczi, 'Freud's "Massenpsychologie und Ich-Analyse. Der individualpsychologische Fortschritt"', in: *Internationale Zeitschrift für Psychoanalyse* 8 (1922/2), p. 206-209, p. 206.

7   S. Freud, *Group Analysis and the Analysis of the Ego* (1921), *SE 18*, pp. 65-143, p. 142.

8   S. Freud, *Group Psychology*, p. 69.

9   J. Rose, 'Introduction', in: S. Freud, *Mass Psychology and Other Writings*. London: Penguin Books 2004, p. vii-xli, p. vii.

10 Elsewhere, for example in the translation of Freud's *The Future of an Illusion*, the term "mass" is translated as "mass" and not as "group".

11 See A. Mitscherlich, 'Massenpsychologie und Ich-Analyse – Ein Lebensalter später', in: *Psyche* 31/6 (1977), pp. 516-539, p. 537.

12 J. Strachey, 'Editor's Note. Massenpsychologie und Ich-Analyse', in: S. Freud, *Group Psychology*, p. 67-68, p. 67.

13 See May in this volume, p. 13 (emphasis added).

14 See S. Winter, 'Aber Wien darf nicht deutsch werden', in: M. Brunner, H. D. König, J. König & J. Lohl (eds.), *Sozialpsychologie der Massenbildung. 100 Jahre Sigmund Freuds "Massenpsychologie und Ich-Analyse"*. Wiesbaden: Springer 2022, pp. 5-60, p. 37

15 T. W. Adorno, 'Freudian Theory and the Pattern of Fascist Propaganda', in: G. Róheim (Ed.), *Psychoanalysis and the Social Sciences*, Vol. 3, New York: International Universities Press, 1951, pp. 279-300.

16 See Maani in this volume, p. 99.

17 See Newman in this volume, p. 165.

18 P. Bump, 'Why Trump is winning, as shown in Wednesday night's dueling programming', in: Washington Post, January 11, 2024. https://www.washingtonpost.com/politics/2024/01/11/trump-dishonesty-presidential-election/ (accessed 02-02-2024).

19 Fred McFeely Rogers (1928–2003), known as Mister Rogers, a legendary American children's television host, whose series *Mister Rogers' Neighborhood* ran from 1968 to 2001.

20 S. Freud, *Group Psychology*, p. 79.

21 T. S. Eliot, 'The Tradition and the Individual Talent', in: *The Egoist* VI/4 (1919), p. 54-55, p. 54.

Sexual Drives, Eros, and Identification – A Re-reading of Freud's *Group Psychology and the Analysis of the Ego*[1]

Ulrike May

Freud's *Group Psychology and the Analysis of the Ego*[2] is such a rich text that I have taken the liberty of reacting to only a few select aspects. I will start with some reflections on the genesis of the text; after that, I shall discuss the meaning and significance of "identification", arguably the core concept underlying *Group Psychology*.

In *Group Psychology and the Analysis of the Ego*, Freud turned his attention to phenomena observable in groups and "masses" of adults: regression, ego paralysis, and the like. His primary goal was *not* to describe mass-specific phenomena or to call attention to additional phenomena not yet described. Freud was after something else. He wanted to be able to identify the infantile roots of these phenomena. Remarkably, he did not draw on earlier conceptualizations of the individual and his/her relationships within the family, such as the Oedipus complex. On the contrary, Freud put those previously developed concepts to the side, offering fresh ideas and theories about group specific dynamics. He obviously felt that the processes taking place in a mass were processes *sui generis*, that is to say, of a completely different nature than oedipal ones. It is, I believe, evidence of Freud's brilliance that he repeatedly risked articulating perceptions that initially did not fit the current state of his theorizing, permitting him to change his theories frequently. *Group Psychology and the Analysis of the Ego* is no exception to this 'rule'. Here, the changes concern mainly the theory of normal psychic development, especially ego development. Also affected, albeit marginally, are clinical theory and metapsychology which I shall not go into.

Ulrike May

On the Genesis of Group Psychology and the Analysis of the Ego

Reconstructing the genesis of published texts has fallen out of fashion; perhaps it was never really 'en vogue'. These days, there are only a handful of researchers who work that way.[3] To be sure, at first glance, the process seems somewhat drab and pedantic, but, as I hope to be showing, new connections can be brought to light, new insights can be gained.

Group Psychology and the Analysis of the Ego appeared in 1921, after *Beyond the Pleasure Principle* (1920) and before *The Ego and the Id* (1923).[4] The text thus belongs to Freud's middle or late writings which mark the transition to the so-called structural model of 1923, with its theory of the dynamics among ego, id, and superego. In what follows I will concentrate on some aspects of this transition.

I begin with the trivial observation that even though Freud significantly changed drive theory when he introduced the death drive and Eros in *Beyond the Pleasure Principle,* in *Group Psychology*, published only a year later, the death drive no longer appears while Eros remains. After reading *Group Psychology*, Max Eitingon wrote to Freud: "Compared with the almost tragic tension of *Beyond*, *Group Psychology* promises so infinitely much that is bright, redemptive, immediately obvious [...]".[5] To Eitingon the two texts seemed quite antithetical. And James Strachey, the editor of the *Standard Edition* and one of the best experts on Freudian theory, writes in the introduction to *Group Psychology*, "There is little direct connection between the present work and its close predecessor, *Beyond the Pleasure Principle*."[6] I have always been puzzled by Strachey's remark as well as by subsequent claims made by scholars who seem to share Strachey's view that, *mutatis mutandis,* after Freud had dealt with the death drives, he turned to the group and the masses. This sounds much too rational to me and does not do justice to Freud's creative process.

My own theory about the connections between *Beyond the Pleasure Principle* and *Group Psychology* is based on the reconstruction of the genesis of *Beyond the Pleasure Principle*.[7] What sparked my interest in the genesis of *Beyond* was Ilse Grubrich-Simitis' discovery of the manuscript of the first draft of *Beyond* in the Freud Archives in Washington, D.C.[8] Michael Schröter and I decided to edit and publish the manuscript.[9]

Freud started writing the first draft of *Beyond the Pleasure Principle* as early as 1919. By mid-April he had completed the manuscript. Surprisingly, it deals exclusively with drives that lead to death. Eros does not make an appearance, neither in name nor in substance.[10] Shortly after the completion of this draft, we find a first mention of a psychoanalytic foundation for group psychology in a letter Freud wrote to Ferenczi on May 12, 1919: "I completed the draft of 'Beyond the Pleasure Principle' [...] and, with a simple-minded idea, I attempted a *Ψα* foundation for group psychology."[11] That is all Freud writes. I shall come back to what he might have meant by "a simple-minded idea".

During the summer vacation of 1919 Freud continued to work on *Beyond the Pleasure Principle*. He was obviously not yet satisfied with what he had put on paper. He read Schopenhauer and was catching up with experimental developmental biology and sexual physiology. At the time, biologists were discussing the conditions under which organisms die. There is a wealth of books and essays from this period on this subject.[12] Freud shared an interest in this kind of work with Ferenczi. Between 1913 and 1918 they exchanged ideas about it frequently and in depth. They also planned a joint publication which, however, did not come to fruition.[13] Instead, Freud wrote the first draft of *Beyond the Pleasure Principle*. Several other papers Freud published during that period also show the mark of his exchange with Ferenczi on the topic of developmental biology and physiology; for example, the January 1920 treatise on female homosexuality,[14] the 4th edition of *Three Essays on the Theory of Sexuality*, and, finally, the revision of the first draft of *Beyond the Pleasure Principle*.

In December 1919 Freud wrote to Max Eitingon: "I am very slowly studying drive and group psychology;" and in March 1920 he wrote: "Meanwhile I am still working on group psychology and death drives."[15] Freud thus continued to think about whether and how he could incorporate the notion of a death drive into his theory while at the same time studying the formation and dynamics of groups and masses. In May 1920 he mentioned that he was planning a "small book" on Group Psychology[16]. Ernest Jones urged him to definitely consider Wilfred Trotter's book on the so-called "herd instinct". Freud replied that he had already read it and that he disagreed with Trotter on two grounds: firstly, the child had no herd instinct; and secondly, he had found a different answer to the question of the origin of the herd instinct. "Paleobiology may intervene even here", he wrote.[17] I shall come back to what Freud might have meant by this reference to paleobiology.

Wilfred Trotter was a British surgeon, a close friend of Ernest Jones and married to Jones' sister. In 1916 his book *The Herd Instinct in War and Peace* had caused a sensation in the UK.[18] By "herd instinct" Trotter meant a biological instinct for group formation and socialization inherent in all organisms. Trotter described different forms of group organization based on biological models. Germany, for example, was organized along the lines of the wolf pack type. Even though he disagreed with some of Trotter's ideas, Freud appreciated the book and devoted an entire chapter to it in *Group Psychology*.[19]

In May 1920, Freud began revising his first draft of *Beyond the Pleasure Principle*. He took the manuscript with him on summer vacation, along with some documents and notes on *Group Psychology*.[20] To his daughter Anna he wrote that he was working on the correction of *Beyond the Pleasure Principle* as well as on the "new treatise" of *Group Psychology*.[21] On July 18, 1920, he announced that *Beyond the Pleasure Principle* was finished; immediately thereafter he began writing the first draft of *Group Psychology,* completing it in just four weeks.[22] We can now answer the question of what Freud meant when he wrote to Jones that the origin of mass or group formation was perhaps to be found in paleobiology. What was meant was the aggregation of unicellular organisms into multicellular organisms brought about by the unifying force of Eros. This first draft of *Group Psychology*, as Freud himself later stated, already contained all the important thoughts of the final version[23], which he completed and submitted for printing in the spring of 1921. We can therefore state that, at the very least, *Group Psychology* was written in the closest temporal proximity with *Beyond the Pleasure Principle*.

Yet the two papers are much more intricately connected. It is important to bear in mind that in the process of writing *Beyond* Freud added an entire chapter to his first draft: namely chapter six in the final version of *Beyond the Pleasure Principle*.[24] He also made changes in the chapters before and after it. This new sixth chapter featured experimental biological research on the death of organisms – as well as Freud's own thoughts on Eros. On page 50 of *Beyond*, as published in volume 18 of the *Standard Edition*, Eros is mentioned as the antagonist of the death drive for the first time and in a context that at first glance seems somewhat strange. Freud raises the question how it is that in the course of evolution unicellular organisms have combined into larger cell groups, i.e. multicellular organisms. The answer he gives is that there must be a force which is responsible for this coalescing. Eros is that force; Eros binds the cells and holds them together. That is Freud's reasoning as to why he incorporated Eros into his theory.[25]

Importantly, Eros is also the main agent of mass formation. In *Group Psychology* as in *Beyond* Freud raises the same question, namely what were the forces that enabled the coalescence of unicellular organisms into multicellular organisms? To answer this question he refers to a "valuable remark of Trotter's, to the effect that the tendency toward the formation of groups is biologically a continuation of the multicellular character of all the higher organisms."[26] Indeed, in his book Trotter had brought this analogy into play several times.[27]

However, he attributed the transition from unicellular to multicellular organisms to a biologically predetermined "herd instinct" while Freud stuck to his own explanation from *Beyond the Pleasure Principle,* claiming that it was Eros that was responsible for the formation of multicellular organisms. We are now in a position to answer the question what Freud meant when he spoke of "a simple-minded idea" on which he based his psychoanalytic theory of mass psychology: it is the analogy between the step from unicellular to multicellular units and that from individual to mass or group formation. And we can now also answer the question what Freud might have meant when he wrote to Jones that the origin of mass formation was perhaps to be found in paleobiology. What Freud was alluding to was the merging of unicellular organisms into multicellular organisms in the course of the evolutionary history of organisms.

Freud may have taken the analogy from Trotter, or perhaps he just found it a confirmation of his own speculations. What is certain, though, is that not only in terms of their genesis *Beyond the Pleasure Principle* and *Group Psychology* belong closely together, albeit in a highly speculative way. It has also become clear that initially Freud was trying to find a way to accommodate the idea that there are drives that strive toward death (the main idea of the first version of *Beyond*) and that he then, in a second step, introduced Eros as the counterpart of the death drives, a theoretical move that enabled him to take into account biological and psychological processes of "higher development", namely the the combining of cellular units as well as the development of the individual into a being capable of forming "groups".

As will become clear in a moment, Freud was of the opinion that in the beginning the baby is a kind of anti-social being and only later shows the capacity to form "masses" or "groups", starting with the capacity to identify with a parent. In this respect, for Freud *Group Psychology* was probably a kind of continued engagement with *Beyond the Pleasure Principle.* So much so that he not even mentioned the death drives in *Group Psychology.* Clearly, Freud envisioned mass or group formation as a process in which the death drives were not actively involved. That groups, once they exist, might develop hostile attitudes toward each other is another matter. In *Group Psychology* Freud discusses these processes which he understood to be possible only after the death drive had turned towards objects outside of the ego/organism.[28] This 'turning towards the outside', as Freud conceived it, is carried out by Eros which thereby transforms the death drives into aggressive drives for the purpose of protecting the organism or the individual from self-destruction.[29]

Ulrike May

Freud famously appreciated the rationales of developmental biology and he took a great interest in what was then called 'history of humankind' ("Menschheitsgeschichte"). At the time, both were state of the art approaches whereas nowadays we tend to disregard them, perhaps even with a sense of embarrassment, as they no longer fit our thinking. Today, when we want to conceptualize the "cohesion" of people, we speak of a we-feeling, of group identities, group cohesion, the group matrix, or of the archaic need for similar objects, of alter ego and twinship transference. Like Freud, we have similar phenomena in mind. Unlike him, we do not refer to ancient philosophy and evolutionary biology. But perhaps in future times people will be as bewildered by our conceptual tools and repertoire of images as we are at Freud's.

On Pre-Oedipal Identification

Identification, which is the subject of the seventh chapter of *Group Psychology*, is at the heart of the entire text. The chapter begins with "Identification is known to psycho-analysis as the earliest expression of an emotional tie with another person."[30] A remarkable sentence for two reasons. First of all, it is not accurate, I think, for nowhere had Freud said anything along those lines before; nothing of the sort was "known". Secondly, one is surprised to read that Freud describes identification as an "emotional tie" ("Gefühlsbindung"), even an "earliest" one. We are not used to such "soft" language from Freud. And why does he speak of an "emotional tie" rather than a "libidinal" tie or a libidinal relationship? Here's how Freud continues,

> it [identification] plays a part in the early history of the Oedipus com-
> plex[31]. A little boy will exhibit a special interest in his father; he would
> like to grow like him and be like him, and take his place everywhere.
> We may say simply that he takes his father as his ideal.[32]

I have always found the first pages of the seventh chapter of *Group Psychology* to be special: simple, direct, substantial, and phrased in a way that is neither alienating nor outdated. In the few lines quoted here, Freud leaves no doubt that firstly, he is talking about pre-oedipal identifications (as opposed to post-oedipal ones); and secondly, these identifications are psychological processes that are not identical with libidinal relations or a libidinal cathexis. Freud explicitly affirms this a few lines further on, and moreover indicates that identifications precede libidinal investment; they are the genetically

26

earlier mode of relating. Further on, Freud describes the difference between identification and libidinal object cathexis: in the case of identification, the object is what one wants to be; in the case of a libidinal object relation, the object is what one wants to have.[33]

Rarely has Freud described the difference between libidinal object relations and identifications as clearly as in this passage. It is immediately obvious: a libidinal object cathexis, paradigmatically the Oedipal one, implies urgent desires, a wanting to possess, to have for oneself, to fulfill longing and desiring, and bring it to rest. An identificatory relationship means something calmer, something which does not push for any final action and does not bring tension-relieving satisfaction. If the boy wants to become like father, this 'I want to become (like) you' is not an imperative drive-based impulse in the strict sense of the word. How the difference can be theorized, however, remains unclear. Freud speaks at some length of identification brought about by Eros as being goal-inhibited or sublimated energy. This is, I think, unconvincing, since we are dealing with early, pre-oedipal processes. Does it really make sense to assume that early processes work with inhibited energy while later ones work with uninhibited energy? Freud himself admits the difficulties of theorization.[34]

We, thus, encounter the problem of how the sexual drives and Eros relate to one another. In several of his texts, including "An outline of psycho-analysis", one of his last papers, Freud states that the sexual drives are to be subsumed under Eros.[35] Similarly, in *Group Psychology* he subsumes libidinal object cathexis and identificatory processes under the concept of "emotional ties." As I have illustrated in an earlier publication, at this point the weighty and consequential question arises whether the two processes really have a common denominator.[36] As Freud had argued in *Three Essays on the Theory of Sexuality*, the main characteristic of infantile sexuality was its objectlessness, its auto-eroticism. Although Freud subsequently modified this somewhat, he always upheld that the baby or very young child was primarily interested in gratification. Babies have, as Freud presented it in *Group Psychology*, no "herd instinct". Only gradually is the child able to show concern for the love object and its wishes; only gradually will it do something for the sake of the object. This, after all, constitutes the lifelong power of infantile impulses: they insist on their gratification heedlessly and undiscerning. But this striving for gratification, I think, cannot be reconciled with the aims of Eros: Eros strives to bind together, to coalesce individuals into larger units, to hold everything together – which is precisely something that cannot be said of the small child.

If, indeed, Eros was difficult to reconcile with infantile sexuality, what would that mean? Was the Freud from after 1920, after *Beyond the Pleasure Principle* and after *Group Psychology*, no longer who he used to be before? Did he himself abandon the discovery of infantile sexuality? Certainly not. As we have seen, infantile sexuality has been preserved in the concept of "libidinal cathexis of the object". Moreover, the reports from analyses we have of Freud's patients from after 1920 show that Freud held on to his 1905 conceptualization of infantile sexuality. And yet, in *Beyond* as well as in *Group Psychology* he placed Eros and identification alongside the sexual drives. Both are regarded as significant for psychic development as the libidinal impulses themselves.

This is to be understood, I think, as meaning that Freud's theorizing had been changing direction for some time without him actually intending this change in direction. From about 1913/1914 on, Freud increasingly had ideas that went beyond the libido theory; ideas that could no longer be reconciled with it. The conceptualization of Eros and the death drive was, perhaps, the last manifestation of his thinking guided by the sexual theory he had developed in 1905. Freud was moving, I believe, in the direction of the ego, and *Group Psychology* was one stop along the way, its title explicitly referring to the "Analysis of the Ego".

Of course, Freud had always spoken of the ego and also repeatedly of identifications. Even before 1921, Freud used the concept of "ego parts" that were in conflict with one another, observed and judged each other, or were identified with objects; and there was a whole bundle of ego functions, such as reality testing, defense, access to motility, or ego deformations, such as narcissistic grandiosity. Until 1921 his attempts at conceptualizing the ego remained isolated efforts, stemming from his analyses of various clinical observations. In *Group Psychology* his efforts condensed into the concept of the now assumed to be normal early pre-oedipal identification, a concept Freud retained and elaborated on in *The Ego and the Id*. The early identifications and ideal formations constituted, as Freud says in *Group Psychology*, a developmental stage of the ego. This gave the ego a developmental history that was more substantial and tangible than in any previous attempt.

By all means, in 1921 identification was not a new concept. Freud had long spoken of hysterical identification, of male homosexuality as an identification with the mother, and of the totemic meal as an identification of the adult brothers with the father. In 1915, while thinking about the etiology of depression, he discovered a narcissistic type of identification with the lost or disappointing object.[37] All this, however, had not yet come together. It seems that it was only in *Group Psychology* that Freud arrived at the normal variant of identification, namely, the pre-oedipal "tender" identification with the parental object. Then, in *The Ego and the Id*, to mention it briefly, he added the post-oedipal identifications as normal resolutions of the oedipal conflict. If what I have postulated here could be confirmed, *Group Psychology and the Analysis of the Ego* would be the piece of writing in which Freud returned, so to speak, to normality, that is, to a conceptualization of normal psychic development after he had grasped the abysses of narcissistic identification in depression and schizophrenia, and had dealt with the equally disturbing death drives, the central forces of self-destruction.

Translated from German by Bettina Mathes

Notes

1 Slightly revised version of paper given on June 10, 2022 at the Sigmund Freud Museum Vienna.
2 S. Freud, *Group Analysis and the Analysis of the Ego* (1921), *SE 18*, pp. 65-143. – Strachey's translation of "Massenpsychologie" as "group psychology" instead of "mass psychology" has been recognized as being misleading by many authors.
3 See, for example, Ph. van Haute & H. Westerink, *Reading Freud's 'Three Essays on the Theory of Sexuality'. From pleasure to the object.* London, New York: Routledge, 2020.
4 S. Freud, *Beyond the Pleasure Principle* (1920), *SE 18*, pp. 1-64; *The Ego and the Id* (1923), *SE 19*, pp. 1-66, 1923.
5 "Gegenüber der geradezu tragischen Spannung des *Jenseits* verheißt die *Massenpsychologie* so unendlich viel Helles, Erlösendes, sofort Einleuchtendes." (S. Freud & M. Eitingon. *Briefwechsel 1906–1939*, Vol. 1. Tübingen: Edition Diskord, 2004; ol. 1, p. 229).
6 J. Strachey, 'Editor's note. Massenpsychologie und Ich-Analyse', *SE 18*, p. 67-69, p. 67.
7 U. May, 'The Third Step in Drive Theory: On the Genesis of "Beyond the Pleasure Principle"', *Psychoanalysis and History* 17 (2015), pp. 205 272.
8 See I. Grubrich-Simitis, *Back to Freud's Texts*. New Haven & London: Yale University Press, pp. 182-191, 1993.
9 U. May & M. Schröter, 'Special Issue: Sigmund Freud, Beyond the Pleasure Principle. New critical edition of manuscript versions, with commentary', in: *Psychoanalysis and History* 17 (2015).
10 Wittels proposed that the introduction of the death drive was partially caused by the death of Freud's daughter Sophie (F. Wittels, *Sigmund Freud: His Personality, His Teaching, and His School.* London: George Allen & Unwin, 1924). As the genesis of *Beyond* shows, Wittel's thesis must be rejected. Sophie died in February

1920, the first draft of *Beyond* was completed by the first half of April 1919, when Sophie was still in good health (U. May, 'The Third Step in Drive Theory: On the Genesis of *Beyond the Pleasure Principle*', in: *Psychoanalysis and History* 17 (2015), p. 208-209).

[11] S. Freud & S. Ferenczi, *The Correspondence of Sigmund Freud and Sandór Ferenczi*, ed. by E. Falzeder, E. Brabant & P. Giamperi-Deutsch, Vol. 2. Cambridge, Mass. London: Belknap Press, 1996, p. 354.

[12] A. Lipschütz, *Warum wir sterben [Why we die]*. Stuttgart: Franckh. See U. May, 'The Third Step', pp. 268-271.

[13] The work to come out of their collaboration was *A Phylogenetic Fantasy. Overview of the Transference Neuroses*, ed. I. Grubrich-Simitis. Cambridge, MA: The Belknap Press of Harvard University Press, 1987, written in 1915 and published posthumously (1987).

[14] S. Freud, 'The psychogenesis of a case of female homosexuality' (1929), *SE* 18, pp. 147-172.

[15] S. Freud & M. Eitingon, *Briefwechsel 1906–1939*. Tübingen: Edition diskord (2004), vol. 1, p. 176, 194.

[16] *The Complete Correspondence of Sigmund Freud and Karl Abraham 1907–1925. Completed edition*. Transcribed and edited by E. Falzeder. London & New York: Karnac, 2002, p. 423.

[17] S. Freud & E. Jones, *The Complete Correspondence 1908–1939*, ed. R.A. Paskauskas. Cambridge, MA & London: The Belknap Press of Harvard University Press (1993), p. 373.

[18] W. Trotter, *The Herd Instinct in War and Peace*. London: Adelphi Terrace, 1916. The second edition, printed in 1919, contained a tirade of hate against Germany which Freud found rather unfortunate (*Group Psychology*, p. 118).

[19] S. Freud, *Group Psychology*, pp. 117-121.

[20] S. Freud & K. Abraham, *Complete Correspondence*, p. 427.

[21] S. Freud & A. Freud, *Correspondence 1904–1938*, ed. by I. Meyer-Palmedo. Cambridge: Polity Press, 2024, p. 186.

[22] S. Freud & M. Eitingon, *Briefwechsel 1906–1939*, p. 213; S. Freud & A. Freud, *Correspondence*, p. 195.

[23] S. Freud & S. Ferenczi, *The Correspondence of Sigmund Freud and Sandór Ferenczi*, Vol. 3, p. 60.

[24] S. Freud, *Beyond*, pp. 44-61.

[25] S. Freud, *Beyond*, p. 50.

[26] S. Freud, *Group Psychology*, p. 87.

[27] See, for example, W. Trotter, *The Herd Instinct*, 2nd edition (1919), p. 103.

[28] S. Freud, *Group Psychology*, pp. 101-14, 110. – The German "Wendung nach außen" refers to the death drive aiming at something that lies outside ("außerhalb") the ego and/or outside ("außerhalb") the organism, which is to say, at objects not identical with the ego or the organism.

[29] The whole argument is presented in S. Freud, *Beyond*, p. 50 f.

[30] See S. Freud, *Group Psychology*, p. 105.

[31] "Early history" is a somewhat misleading translation. The German version has "Vorgeschichte" (pre-history), conveying that Freud attributed processes of identification to the period before the Oedipus complex.

[32] Ibid.

[33] S. Freud, ibid., p. 106.

[34] According to Freud identifications are "insufficiently-known processes and hard to describe" (S. Freud, *Group Psychology*, p. 104). And in a similar vein: "It is much more difficult to give a metapsychological representation of the distinction" (ibid, p. 106). In the 'Postscript' Freud continues to struggle with solving this problem. In my view, he does not arrive at a convincing solution (ibid., pp. 134-143).

[35] S. Freud, 'An Outline of Psycho-Analysis' (1940 [1938]), *SE* 23, pp. 141-207.

[36] U. May, 'The Third Step', pp. 250-252.

[37] U. May, '"Das Objekt verdunkelt das Ich." Victor Tausks und Karl Landauers Beiträge zum Begriff der narzisstischen Identifizierung im Entwurf von Freuds 'Trauer und Melancholie', in: *Jahrbuch der Psychoanalyse* 72 (2016), pp. 173-208; U. May, 'In Conversation: Freud, Abraham and Ferenczi on "Mourning and Melancholia" (1915–1918)', in: *International Journal of Psychoanalysis* 100 (2019), pp. 77-98.

Freud's "Mass Psychology"*

Helmut Dahmer

We live in the age of "positivism," the restrictive instrumentalization of reason[1], which has taken hold of psychoanalysis as well. The telos of Freudian therapeutics was "liberation from unnecessary inner compulsion" (Ferenczi)[2], but in the course of their pragmatic turn, the vast majority of psychoanalysts have dispensed with the Freudian negation of existing civilization[3] and have made therapeutic technique, *a means* for the cognition of unconscious processes, *the main concern*. Consequently, psychoanalysis has been misunderstood – especially by sociologists and social psychologists – as an instrument of social control (Talcott Parsons) and the Freudian formula of mass bonding as an organizational prescription,[4] while doctors and psychologists, who claimed Freud's legacy, left his drive- and culture-theories aside. The Freudians who had fled Hitler's Germany, like their colleagues in the Western countries of refuge, had lost their (political) language due to Hitler's and Stalin's cannibalistic regimes. Apart from the one Wilhelm Reich[5] (whom they excluded because of this), they kept silent about Hitler's (totalitarian) mass movement, their enemy. "Group Psychology and the Analysis of the Ego" could have shone a light on fascism (before, just as after 1933), but – in contrast to Adorno (1951) – they did not know what to do with it...[6]

"Masses", "Free" Wage Workers, the Self-Employed, and Dependents

Critically following the publications of the mass psychologists Gustave Le Bon (1892), Wilfred Trotter (1916), and William McDougall (1920), Freud (1921) characterized "the life of an individual man of to-day" as follows:

> Each individual is a component part of numerous groups, he is bound by ties of identification in many directions, and he has built up his ego ideal upon the most various models. Each individual, therefore, has a share in numerous group minds – those of his race, of his class, of his

creed, of his nationality, etc. – and he can also raise himself above them to the extent of having a scrap of independence and originality.[7]

The situation of the individuals described here, who can at least "rise a little" above the masses they take part in, is modern ("today's"), and indeed a one that is class-specific. Freud had in mind – like the more historically argumentative sociologist, Georg Simmel – the metropolitan life of the "Belle Époque" and even then, not "everyone" but only members of the classes owning property had access to and a share in "different," even divergent, "masses," in fact, some of them were able to free themselves somewhat from the ties imposed on them by their membership in ethnic, national, religious, and social "groups," and thus were able to *individualize* themselves.

The prerequisite of *this* relationship between masses and individuals, which changed during Freud's lifetime, was the modern, Western European-originated – and, in the course of a few centuries in colonial policy of the major trading and industrialized countries worldwide-expanding – *indirect* socialization of *released* individuals who (have to) participate in the monetarized exchange of goods on markets. This ("capitalist") form of social association was the product of armed civic communities ("military associations") in the typical "occidental" craft and commercial cities of the early modern period, and their success was based on what social historians describe as the "dissolution of feudal allegiances" or "original accumulation": the *dissolution* of village communities, extended families, tribes and estates, and the *detachment* of previously *communalized* individuals from their livelihood, the soil, their separation from the means of life and work – in short, their transformation into unattached "isolated individuals," social atoms who, as far as their labor power is concerned, are *dependent* on the market, i. e. on opportunities for exchange or exploitation. The existence of such a wage labor force (salariat), which is "free" in every respect, is the prerequisite for "rational" economic activity, namely for small and medium-sized enterprises as well as (current day) globally operating corporations.[8] The majority of the earth's population now consists of such "free" wage workers – or their unemployed "reserve army" – and the inhabitants of the old capitalist oases of prosperity in the growing global desert of war and hunger are becoming aware of them, when the desperate refugee vanguard of this majority fails at the walls and fences of Europe and North America or is rescued out of sinking rubber boats in the Mediterranean. These migrants teach us that individuals who were cast out of or sought to break away from the hordes, tribes, estates, guilds, and communities of early (pre-capitalist) "societies," had hardly any chance of survival. Even in Shakespeare's tragedy (written in 1597) of *Romeo and Juliet*, who (in 16ᵗʰ century Verona) prematurely individualized themselves by putting their individual love above the interests of their families, refusing the "arranged marriage," that is, speaking with Freud, they were opting out of the "mass bond" and they paid for it with their lives. Only in modern society are "social atoms" without ties able to survive by selling their labor power; admittedly, their "autonomy" is precarious, dependent on changing market opportunities (business cycles), and their (relative) independence is therefore only existing until revocation.[9]

In the early history of mankind, as well as in pre-civilized, agrarian conditions with a small division of labor – that is, during the longest part of our history – individuals only survived firmly *bound* into certain horde and tribe associations, *fixed* to the territory occupied and used by the association; there were not yet *manifold* "masses" in which they could have participated, and accordingly there was neither the possibility nor the necessity for them – at the intersection of social circles – to become special.[10] With the transition from feudal to bourgeois society, the form of domination or exploitation changed: materially mediated, indirect dependency, namely dependency on production and foods owned by others,[11] took the place of *direct* master-servant relationships. In Hegel's analysis of the relationship between master and servant, the servant ends up (through his labor) on top.[12] But the "free" wage workers have not yet won the struggle for *their* independence even after two centuries of class struggle,[13] while the "self-employed" ("small" and "large") have long since become a minority. We live in a *society of dependent workers*.

Freud's formulation of the relationship of the individual (or individuals) to the "masses" in which they participate and by which they are carried – respectively to their psychic "representations" which overlap and intersect in the construction of their "ego ideal" – is an index of a certain social situation: the "bourgeois" revolutions (with the support of the propertyless plebians) had increased private property and created a new, large class of "self-employed" in town and country by expropriating and parceling out the noble and ecclesiastical large-scale property. A hundred years before Freud, poets and philosophers had glorified the (relative) independence of the isolated individuals, namely the owners of land, capital, or even just labor power, and had elevated *autonomy* to a cultural ideal. In Fichte's solipsistic *Wissenschaftslehre* (from 1794), an autonomous, self-conscious, free "Ego" – be it the individual or the societal – in the process of its reflection (as an "action") produced (or "set") both itself and the Non-Ego, the world – that is, subject and object – which presuppose each other.[14] Yet in the "long" 19th century, the century of industrialization, competition among private owners led to the concentration of capital, and more and more individuals lost their economic independence and became (again) dependents. Individuality lost its economic basis.[15] In everyday practice, like in ideology, the loss of autonomy and de-individualization ("collectivization") took the place of autonomization and individualization.

After the experience of the material battles, gas and trench warfare of World War I, the "Ego" emerged on the Freudian map of the (modern) soul as a mere province of the continent of the unconscious, although crucial for the survival of individuals. The instance which is responsible for perception and consciousness in the psychic household, appears as an artist of compromise, dependent on the energies of other "instances": as a Chaplinesque clown who only *fakes* autonomy anymore, by claiming that everything that happens to him in the circus of life is arranged by him in advance and is under his control.[16] In accordance with this "metapsychological" finding, the individuals struggling for "a bit of independence" no longer appear in Freud's 1921 "sociology" as masters of themselves and their world, but rather as drowning people who are just barely keeping their heads above water, who could be swallowed up at any moment by the waves of the mass sea both within and outside them.[17]

Primordial Hordes: History of Revolutions and Archaic Heritage

"Battles that are old history are new to us,
and one's neighbor rushes in with a jubilant face to tell the news."
—Franz Kafka[18]
"The legacy of the dead generations weighs
like an alp upon the brains of the living."
—Karl Marx[19]

I think that the "discontent" of individuals subjected to cultural development, namely to the (modern) process of their progressive dispossession and their transformation into dependent employees, induced Freud to pursue the "feebleness of the ego" he had registered metapsychologically also in the sociological field – which he considered to be one of "applied psychology."[20] From the authorities of social psychology of that time, he adopted the term "mass" ("herd," "group") for *all* forms of communal *and* social human aggregates in history and present, in both the European and non-European worlds. Not the leaderless pack or "herd" (of whose fates nothing is known), but the "horde" led by a tyrannical lord over life and death, the "primal father"-shepherd, was regarded by him as the prototype (or "original phenomenon") of human communalization. It was already psychologically, even "mass-psychologically," structured, and that means that it was characterized by the tense relationship between the *two* "psychologies," namely the "individual" one of the despotic, "free," and also sexually unrestricted primal father, and that of the sons, who were condemned by him to a sexual abstinence or homosexuality (or even castrated by him), who feared him (and identified themselves with him and their brothers). The tension of the two "psychologies" eventually led to the disruption of the patriarchal structure. Revolutionary fraternization (and sisterhood) enabled the (now fatherless, freed from the tyrant) horde members a phase of free sexual relations, perhaps also a "matriarchy," but then, longing for the father (attachment to the former "group ideal") and a sense of guilt, urged the sons to "belated obedience" and the re-establishment of patriarchy. The history of the hordes was thus subject to the compulsion to repeat, even if the repetition of the cycle might result in variations and sublimations over time.

Freud's patriarchal male-bonding "scientific myth,"[21] his *narrative* of human pre- or early history, as it may have occurred, occupied Freud for a quarter of a century and is found in three versions (essentially identical in content).[22] His reconstruction joins together three components: Darwin's concept of "Primal Horde,"[23] Atkinson's hypothesis of "brotherly revolt" (1903), and Robertson Smith's depiction of the ritual "totem-meal" (1889) as a feast of remembrance of revolt, of the triumph of the sons, and of the incorporation of the primordial father they had slain together.[24]

It touches strangely that Freud in 1921 in his "Mass Psychology" did not say a word about the mass phenomena of his time – to the war-enthusiastic, nationalistically fanatic masses of 1914, to the masses of soldiers who endured four years of deadly obedience on the fronts of the war, to the mutinous revolutionary masses of 1918, or to the self-governing organizations of the workers' and soldiers' councils[25] – in which (in 1919) one of his first Viennese colleagues, Paul Federn, saw the model of a brotherhood of the future,[26] – nor to the masses that the counter-revolution mustered against the revolters, or to the horrific (anti-"Bolshevik") Jewish pogroms that raged in Ukraine in 1918–1921. Instead, he referred – like his social-psychological predecessors – to the peripetia of the French Revolution, namely to the succession of "regimes" that followed it: initially, the absolute *monarchy* was overthrown by the democratic uprising of the "third" estate under the slogan "liberty, equality, *fraternity*" (1789). The "fourth" class, the Sansculottes, actively supported Girondists and Jacobins and became, as the fate of Babeuf's "conspiracy for equality" (1796/97) demonstrates, soon deprived of power. But at first the "National Assembly" was followed by the elected, constitutional "Assembly" (the "National Convention"), the war against internal (Vendée) and external enemies, the killing of the monarch (1793) and the Jacobin terror, the reaction of the Thermidor (1794) and, at the end of the cycle, the coronation of the revolutionary general Napoléon as emperor.

Freud's history of "mass psychology," therefore, is actually a condensed history of the course of the English and French revolutions of the 17th and 18th centuries – transposed into (or projected onto) early human history. In ancient times, the two psychologies, that of the despot and libertine and that of the horde members, oppressed by him and kept in double bondage, that is, "authoritarian," evolved into existence. The history of mankind has since been under the spell of this prehistoric, culture-founding acquisition, and, according to Ernst Haeckel's "biogenetic law" (1866), according to which ontogenesis is a shortened, condensed repetition of the phylogenesis of the species, every human child has to pass through a compressed version of the primordial horde history in *their* early days in the fold of the family. It is essentially a history of despotic regimes (the basis of which is the double bond between the followers and the despot) and anti-authoritarian democratic rebellions, and the two replace each other in (seemingly) infinite succession. This sequence, determining the destiny of the primitive hordes – like that of the masses of the present – has sedimented itself namely as "archaic heritage" in the biological equipment of our species. Freud's thesis of the "archaic heritage" (deposited in the "Id") corresponds to Noam Chomsky's postulate of an innate "generative grammar," without which child language acquisition is inexplicable.[27] In this "universal grammar," "the formal properties of every possible human language" are determined a priori.[27] This "universal grammar" needs to be *awakened* by linguistic stimuli ("data") and once updated, provides the child with a "knowledge" that reaches immeasurably far beyond his or her experience. By virtue of this general knowledge, he is able to "discover" or "reinvent" the grammar of the specific language (of his milieu).[28] Analogously – with Freud – it would have to be assumed that every individual latently possesses the entire ensemble of psychological modes ("heritage of emotions", "Gefühlserbschaften"),[29] that is, attitudes and capacities to act, which were acquired in the prehistory of hordes and communities (as a result of "traumas") and since then have been *inherited* in the chain of generations.[30] It then depends on the milieu-specific "stimuli" which of these modes – or which phase of human prehistory – is "awakened" (or actualized) collectively and life-historically, that is, whether the mass individuals tend rather to submission or subversion, to submit their fate or to rebel against it. Once again it becomes clear that "ego strength" or weakness – just like the "principle of reality" – are *social historical* categories which appear in Freud's metapsychology in the form of power relations of the psychic "instances" (or, in the case of the "principle of reality," as an *intrapsychic* regulatory principle).[31] And it also becomes understandable, why Freud was particularly interested in the two phases of mass psychology before patricide and after the dissolution of the (democratic) "community of brothers" – that is, the phases before and after a certain individualization (and democratization) of the members of the horde – in the sequence of the repeating fates of the hordes and clans. The threatening relapse to pre-individual (pre-bourgeois) social relations, to conformist masses, their delusion, their subservience and murderousness, was the (old familiar) "uncanny"[32] that deeply worried him, and the search for a way out (or exit) from the (new-old) mass bondage, led him (1921) to write his treatise. The rebellious brothers and sisters of 1918 were already defeated by then, and the mass hostile mass-movements of the disillusioned, frightened, and desperate, went in search of leaders, demagogues and potential despots who would enable them to act out their hatred.[33]

Ways Out of Mass Psychology

Freud's attitude towards the "masses" is (like Le Bon's) ambivalent. Indeed, he occasionally acknowledges their achievements,[34] but then, in the style of a colonizer, he says that they are indolent and without insight,[35] and that genial "great men" – such as the Pharaoh Akhenaten and his successors (Moses and the prophets) – are needed to impose on them renunciations of instinct ("progress in spirituality").[36] In anomic or crisis situations, individuals regress; they reactivate infantile or "primitive" behavior patterns that lie ready in their "archaic heritage" and abandon themselves to the deindividualizing pull of the masses: "what is heterogeneous is submerged in what is homogeneous."[37] They willingly submit to the "new authority" of the masses, which appears to them to represent the whole of human society, suspend their individualized conscience, and mutate into will-less "automaton[s]".[38]

The anti-authoritarian, egalitarian motive that drove Freud to search for ways to resist or escape the de-individualizing mass pull becomes apparent in an account – included in *Group Psychology* – of his experience with the hypnosis procedure practiced by Hippolyte Bernheim[39]:

> From McDougall we hear as well as from other writers that groups are distinguished by their special suggestibility. We shall therefore be prepared for the statement that suggestions (or more correctly suggestibility) are actually an irreducible, primitive phenomenon, a fundamental fact in the mental life of man. Such, too, was the opinion of Bernheim, of whose astonishing arts I was a witness in the year 1889. But I can remember even then feeling a muffled hostility to this tyranny of suggestion. When a patient who showed himself unamenable was met with the shout: 'What are you doing? *Vous vous contre-suggestionnez*', I said to myself that this was an evident injustice and an act of violence. For the man certainly had a right to counter-suggestions if people were trying to subdue him with suggestions. Later on, my resistance took the direction of protesting against the view that suggestion, which explained everything, was itself to be exempt from explanation.[40]

How a member of the primal hunter-gatherer horde managed to rise to the position of a despot and owner of a harem, is not explained in Freud's construction (or legend) of early man. One can assume that in each case it was the best hunter, toolmaker (perhaps painter, storyteller, or magician). In any case, Freud describes him as the first "free man" who had all others as his property, presumably advanced to a non-"worker" and claimed all women for the satisfaction of his urges, while he imposed heterosexual asceticism on his – now "unfree" – male competitors within the horde. In the event of his death, the youngest of his sons became his successor. The sons (who formed the "first mass"), fraternally bound to each other by homosexually tinged, purpose-restrained sexuality, finally conspired against the forefather, whom they both revered and hated, killing him and consuming him in order to partake of his mysterious power. With one blow there were now many "free", men as well as women, and during the "fatherless time" the women of the horde were enabled to gain the upper hand ("matriarchy"). Yet then, paternal longing and a sense of guilt drove sons and daughters to restore the old order and deferred obedience to the original father and the "incest taboo" (or the complementary exogamy commandment) he had imposed. "The male became once more the chief of the family and broke down the prerogatives of the gynecocracy which had become established during the fatherless period."[41] Thus came about the formation of the "totemic clan," the appointment of sacred animal as the substitute of the (murdered) primal father, and the foundation of a periodically repeated feast of reconciliation and unification of the clan members, in which the "liberating" atrocity of the (common) patricide was repeated by the sacrifice of the totemic animal, and the identification with the father-substitute was renewed by its consumption. But "the new family was only a shadow of the old; there were numbers of fathers and each one was limited by the rights of the others." (ibid.) At this point, Freud introduces the (psychological) "hero myth" as a (further, different) "step," "by which the individual emerges from group psychology":

> It was then, perhaps, that some individual, in the exigency of his longing, may have been moved to free himself from the group and take over the father's part. He who did this was the first epic poet; and the advance was achieved in his imagination. This poet disguised the truth with lies in accordance with his longing. With the Heros, who alone should have slain the father-monster (to replace him), the poet created the first ego ideal. [...] The lie of the heroic myth culminate[d] in the deification of the hero.[42]

If the lonely despot of the hordes, who had subjugated a human herd, was the first "free" one, the (murderous) band of brothers conquered the freedom from him (and from the renunciation of sex imposed on them by him) for themselves and their tribal sisters, even if in later times they repentantly, in "deferred obedience" ("nachträglichem Gehorsam"), submitted to the "sexual economy" imposed by tyrants, admittedly on a higher level, namely on that of the commandment to seek sexual partners only in "foreign" clans (or tribes). One of the hordes, the first (epic) poet, then glorified the liberator, who was supposed to have slain the father-monster and thus to have accomplished the "detachment from the masses" alone and created with this "heroic myth" of the horde its first ego ideal.

Despots, conspirators, tyrannical murderers (and cannibals), sibling democrats, poets and (Thermidorian) traditionalists thus form the ancestral line of free individuals who more or less set themselves apart from the (diverse) "masses," who were able to escape their spell.[43] Last but not least – and at a late hour in the story[44] – Freud adds to this line the couple in love, a separate "mass of two," which breaks away from the mass horde and flees it:

> Two people coming together for the purpose of sexual satisfaction, in so far as they seek for solitude, are making a demonstration against the herd instinct, the group feeling. The more they are in love, the more completely they suffice for each other.[45]

McDougall had considered how to avoid the psychological disadvantages of group formations (especially the decrease of the intellectual level of group individuals). Oriented to the historical development of "unorganized," pack-like groups into "organized" ones (through stabilization, differentiation based on the division of labor, and the formation of tradition), he suggested that the organized masses of the present should also be brought to such a transformation. Freud made, in the context of his McDougall report, more specifically: "hidden" in this text, a *counterproposal*. He summarized in extreme brevity the social history of the economic and political liberation of the bourgeois individuals from feudal dependence *and* the (subsequent) loss of their independence in the process of transition to the mass society of dependent employees and concluded that the "problem" or the "aim" now consisted in "equip[ping] the group with the attributes of the individual".

> The problem consists in how to procure for the group precisely those features which were characteristic of the individual and which are extinguished in him by the formation of the group. For the individual, outside the primitive group, possessed his own continuity, his self-consciousness, his traditions and customs, his own particular functions and position, and he kept apart from his rivals. Owing to his entry into an 'unorganized' group he had lost this distinctiveness for a time.[46]

"[A]s long as world history follows its logical course, it fails to fulfill its human destiny," wrote Max Horkheimer in the spring of 1940 (in his New York exile).[47] The project that psychoanalysis was supposed to serve was, according to Freud, the advancement of a "civilization no longer oppressive to anyone."[48] A decade after *Group Psychology and the Analysis of the Ego*, he returned to one of the "departures" from mass binding marked in 1921, namely, the "group of two," and wrote: one could "quite well imagine a cultural community consisting of double individuals like this, who, libidinally satisfied in themselves, are connected with one another through the bonds of common work and common interests. If this were so, civilization would not have to withdraw any energy from sexuality." This too, was a foreshadowing of a culture that was no longer "oppressive." Freud's objection, that "civilization" wants to "bind the members of the community together in a libidinal way" and therefore restricts sexual life, is mythological, not sociological. Accordingly, he concludes this passage with the remark that what is still lacking is the insight into "the necessity [...] which forces civilization along this path and which causes its antagonism to sexuality. There must be some disturbing factor which we have not yet discovered."[49]

Coda

Perhaps a history of the "masses" can be described as follows: after the dissolution of communally structured economic units (families and cooperatives), army clusters recruited from "social atoms," factory and forced labor collectives took their place. These "artificial" masses were incapable of satisfying the need for community, which the "isolated individuals" could only satisfy in the private refuge of nuclear families. (The mass worker organizations of the 20th century were interest groups disguised as "communities," managed and directed by functionary cadres.) In the course of capitalist socialization, still existing solidarity communities were marginalized and dissolved. Against this, disoriented and desperate masses protested and still protest, who find no way out of the "housing of bondage" (Max Weber) and therefore fall prey to this or that delusion of salvation. Resourceful demagogues offer themselves to them as prodigious men (or women) – or magicians – and direct their resentment against foreigners, minorities, and "elites." In this way, protest movements are transformed, and terrorist gangs recruited from them ultimately secure the system of rule against which the protests were originally directed. Yet new technologies of "mass communication" (telephone, radio, television, laptops, and smartphones) have created the possibility for a large part of mankind to get in touch with each other at any time – admittedly only in the form of "phantoms," but still in words and pictures – thus (virtually) eliminating the isolation of socialized individuals (and families). Millions of people who have access to the Internet are currently "witnessing" social and natural disasters, riots and demagogy, repression and resistance all over the world – in the deserts of war and poverty as well as in the oases of prosperity. Of course, they remain mute, "soloistic" witnesses in front of their screens or display, powerless as if in dreams. They form a "scattered" mass (Günther Anders) united only by the supply of one and the same information and entertainment material and diverse ideologies. Yet perhaps this new, communicative world network finally opens up the possibility for the formulation of "individuated," enlightened masses – that is, masses without mass delusion – of which revolutionaries like

43

Helmut Dahmer

Kropotkin or Trotsky tell us, and for whose renaissance we have been waiting in vain so far.

Translated from German by Sarah Durkee and revised by Daniela Finzi

Notes

1 M. Horkheimer, *Eclipse of reason*, New York: Bloomsbury, 1947.
2 S. Ferenczi (1908), 'Psycho-Analysis and Education', in: S. Ferenczi, *Final Contributions to the Problems and Methods of Psycho-Analysis*. London: Maresfield Reprint, pp. 280-290, p. 283. Internalized coercion is a function of (a) the average labor productivity achieved in a certain period of social evolution and (b) of the degree of violence used in order to maintain the existing social inequality in this period.
3 "It goes without saying that a civilization which leaves so large a number of its participants unsatisfied and drives them into revolt neither has nor deserves the prospect of a lasting existence." S. Freud (1927), *The Future of an Illusion*, SE 21, pp. 1-56, p. 12.
4 Namely, as a "technique" of embedding individuals into efficient conflict-free teams – like piecework shifts, soccer teams or bomber crews – by making use of the "double bind", as analysed by Freud: The dispense of the individual super-ego and the fraternization with others under the sign of a new, collective super-ego.
5 W. Reich, *The Mass Psychology of Fascism*. A revised version of this book has been translated by Vincent R. Carfagno. New York: Oregon Institute Press, 1946. See H. Dahmer, 'Massenpsychologie des Faschismus. Zur Aktualität von Wilhelm Reichs einzigartiger Analyse von 1933', in: *Avanti*, Mannheim (ISO); Theoriebeilage zur Februar-Nummer, 2000/02, pp. 1-4.
6 "But it is as if the refugee intellectuals have been robbed not only of their citizenship, but also of their minds. [...]. The 'Jewish-Hegelian jargon,' which once carried all the way from London to the German Left [...] now seems completely eccentric. With a sigh of relief they throw away the troublesome weapon [...]." M. Horkheimer (1939), 'The Jews and Europe', in: *Critical Theory and Society. A Reader*. Ed. by S. E. Bronner and D. MacKay Kellner. New York and London: Routledge, pp. 77-99. In contrast to Marx's (London) "jargon", in our case we would have to speak of the Viennese "Schellingian" terminology of Freud. It seems, however, that Freud's essay – 100 years after its publication – is gradually finding the interest it deserves...
7 S. Freud, *Group Psychology*, SE 18, pp. 65-144, p. 129. Freud's contemporary, the sociologist Georg Simmel, formulated the relationship between the individual and society in a similar way: "Every individual exists in the overlapping point of different 'social circles' in which he or she participates; his or her 'originality' results from the specific way of mixing these milieus and of dealing with them." See chapter VI.

('The intersection of social circles'), in: G. Simmel (1908), *Sociology: Inquiries into the Construction of Social Forms*. Transl. by A. J. Blasi, A. K. Jacobs and M. Kanjira-thinkal, Leiden and Boston: Brill, 2009, pp. 262-408.

[8] See also M. Weber (1924), *General Economic History*. Transl. by F. Hyneman, New York: Greenberg, 1927, chapter 4, § 1.

[9] "But human beings become individuals only through the process of history. Man appears originally as a species-being [Gattungswesen], clan being, herd animal – although in no way whatever as a ζῶον πολιτικόν [zoon politicon] in the political sense. Exchange itself is a chief means of this individuation [Vereinzelung]. It makes the herd-like existence superfluous and dissolves it." K. Marx ([1857/1858]), *Grundrisse. Foundations of the critique of political economy (rough draft)*. Harmondsworth: Penguin Books. 1993, p. 420.

[10] "[…] there was only a common will, there were no single ones", S. Freud, *Group Psychology*, p. 121, Fn. 3. See also Marx, *Foundations*, p. 398.

[11] In order to express continuity *and* change of form of domination with *one* term, Marx spoke of "wage slavery" (Lohn-Sklaverei). The "exchange of equivalents" in markets "is only the surface layer of a production which rests on the appropriation of alien labour without exchange, but with the semblance of exchange." Marx, *Foundations*, p. 433.

[12] G. F. Hegel (1807), The *Phenomenology of Spirit*, chapter IV.A. ('Self-Sufficiency and Non-Self-Sufficiency of Self-Consciousness; Mastery and Servitude'). Transl. and edited by T. Pinkard. Cambridge: Cambridge University Press, 2018, pp. 108-116.

[13] Marx summarizes: "Relations of personal dependence […] are the first social forms, in which human productive capacity develops only to a slight extent and at isolated points. Personal independence founded on objective [sachlicher] dependence is the second great form, in which a system of general social metabolism, of universal relations, of all-round needs and universal capacities is formed for the first time. Free individuality, based on the universal development of individuals and on their subordination of their communal, social productivity as their social wealth, is the third stage." Marx, *Foundations*, p. 88.

[14] See on this Horkheimer's 1925/1926-lecture on Fichte, in: *Gesammelte Schriften*, Band 10. Ed. by A. Schmidt. Frankfurt/Main: Fischer 1990, pp. 9-165.

[15] See Horkheimer, *Eclipse of Reason*, chapter IV ('Rise and decline of the individual'), pp. 128-161.

[16] See on this topic S. Freud, 'On the History of the Psycho-Analytic Movement', *SE* 14, pp. 1-66, p. 54.

[17] Le Bon, Freud writes, "has made his brilliant psychological character sketch of the group mind" with regard to "the rapidly formed and transient groups" (to whom "the stable and lasting group formations" stand out less compared to them), and "it is just in these noisy ephemeral groups, which are as it were superimposed upon the others, that we are met by the prodigy of the complete, even though only tempo-rary, disappearance of exactly what we have recognized as individual acquirements." (S. Freud, *Group Psychology*, p. 128.)

[18] F. Kafka, ([1918/19]) 'The Great Wall of China', in: Franz Kafka, *The Great Wall of China and Other Pieces*, London: Secker and Warburg, 1946, p. 81-94, p. 91.

[19] K. Marx (1852), *The Eighteenth Brumaire of Louis Bonaparte*. Transl. by E. & C. Paul. London: George Allen & Unwin, 1926, p. 23.

[20] S. Freud, *New Introductory Lectures On Psycho-Analysis*, SE 22, pp. 1-182, p. 179.

[21] This is indeed a purely male story; the "matriarchy" only comes into play as a (comparatively) short-lived by-product of the overthrow of the father. See S. Freud, *Totem and Taboo*, SE 13, pp. vii-162, p. 143; S. Freud, *Group Psychology*, p. 154; S. Freud, *Moses and Monotheism*, SE 23, pp. 1-138, p. 83.

[22] Namely, in the fourth part of *Totem and Taboo* (1912/1913); in the chapter "The Group and the Primal Horde" of *Group Psychology and the Analysis of the Ego* (1921) and in the third part, section "Application" of *Moses and Monotheism* (1937–1939).

[23] C. Darwin, *The descent of man*. London: John Murray, 1871, chapter 20.

[24] In a revealing letter to Ralf L. Worrall, Freud wrote (on 10 September 1937): "For the evidence of the assumption about the human horde I must [...] refer to my warrantors Darwin and Atkinson. [...] Of course, I only accepted the theory of these authors because they corresponded so well with the impressions and expectations from psychoanalytical experience." https://www.loc.gov/resource/mss39990.04404/?sp=2&r=-0.653,-0.022,2.307,1.371,0n (accessed 02-09-2023).

[25] See H. Hautmann, *Geschichte der Rätebewegung in Österreich*, 1918–1924. Vienna: Europa-Verlag 1987; F. Klopotek, *Rätekommunismus. Geschichte – Theorie*. Stuttgart: Schmetterling-Verlag, 2021.

[26] In 1919, Paul Federn saw in the council organisations not only a new "brotherly revolt", but the model of a new society freed from authoritarian father dictatorship and patricide, consisting of brothers in solidarity (or "all fathers"). See H. Dahmer, 'Psychoanalyse und Rätebewegung', *Internationale Zeitschrift für Sozialpsychologie und Gruppendynamik in Wirtschaft und Gesellschaft* 45/2 (2020), pp. 3-18. In his enthusiasm, Federn forgot not only the sisters and mothers of the horde, but also the – for Freud central – longing for the father and the feeling of guilt of the "parricidal" horde of brothers, which compels them to "retrospective obedience" – to "psychic thermidor".

[27] Freud also refers to the circumstance that "[t]he symbolic representation of one object by another [...] is familiar to all our children and comes to them, as it were, as a matter of course"; and that one "must admit that in many cases" it is not a learned skill, but "the 'innate' symbolism which derives from the period of the development of speech, which is familiar to all children without their being instructed, and which is the same among all peoples despite their different languages." S. Freud, *Moses and Monotheism*, p. 98 and 132.

[28] The empirical problem, as Chomsky puts it, is "that no one has been able to devise an initial hypothesis rich enough to account for the acquisition by the child of the grammar that we are, apparently, led to attribute to him when we try to account for his ability to use the language in the normal way. [...]. In short, the language is 'reinvented' each time it is learned". N. Chomsky, *Language and Mind*. Third Edition. New York: Cambridge University Press, 2006, p. 76.

[29] S. Freud, *Totem and Taboo*, p. 159.

[30] Ferenczi's book *Thalassa. An Attempt at a Genital Theory* (1924 [1934]) was the result of his reflections, discussed with Freud, on what he called "bioanalysis", a "Lamarckian" oriented hermeneutics of nature. If the evolution of species was provoked by geological-climatic "catastrophes" that forced more or less successful adaptations, birth and coitus could be understood as their repetition (in the course of "thalassal regression"): The phylogenetic emergence of organic life returns ontogenetically in the maturation of the gametes; the beginning of sexual reproduction in fertilization; species development in the sea as embryonal development in the womb; adaptation to land life as birth; the development of mating organs in the development of genital primacy.

[31] H. Dahmer (1973), *Libido und Gesellschaft. Studien über Freud und die Freudsche Linke*. 3., erweiterte Auflage. Münster: Westfälisches Dampfboot, 2013, part I, chapter 4, pp. 180-193.

[32] The result of his study on 'The Uncanny': "this uncanny is in reality nothing new or alien, but something which is familiar and old-established in the mind and which has become alienated from it only through the process of repression." S. Freud, 'The Uncanny' (1919), *SE* 17, pp. 217-256, p. 241.

[33] Perhaps the manuscript H on "paranoia" attached to his letter to W. Fliess of 24 January 1895 was the seed of Freud's theory of delusion and mass delusion: "Paranoia," he wrote, was a "question of abuse of a psychic mechanism that is very commonly employed in normal life: transposition, or projection. [...] The *grande nation* cannot face the idea that it could be defeated in war. Ergo it was not defeated, the victory does not count. It provides an example of mass paranoia and invents the delusion of betrayal. [...] In every instance the delusional idea is maintained with the same energy with which another, intolerably distressing, idea is warded off from the ego. Thus they *love their delusions as they love themselves*. That is the secret." (p. 110 f.) *The Complete Letters of Sigmund Freud to Wilhelm Fliess*. 1887–1904. J. M. Masson (Ed.). Cambridge, MA: The Belknap Press of Harvard University Press, 1985, p. 109 f.

[34] In this context, Freud distinguishes short-lived, enthusiastic, revolutionary masses from the "stable groups or associations in which mankind pass their lives, and which are embodied in the institutions of society." (S. Freud, *Group Psychology*, p. 83). Revolutionary masses (as they appeared in the French Revolution) moralize (according to Le Bon) the individuals by turning them away from the exclusive pursuit of private interests. In general, "the masses" are capable of great achievements, of ingenious intellectual creations such as language, folklore, etc.

[35] See Chapter II ("Le Bon's Description") of Freud's *Group Psychology*, in which he approvingly refers to Le Bon's remarks (which he says correspond to his own psychology) "that when individuals come together in a group all their individual inhibitions fall away and all the cruel, brutal and destructive instincts, which lie dormant in individuals as relics of a primitive epoch, are stirred up to find free gratification." (p. 79)

[36] See S. Freud, *Moses and Monotheism*, SE 23, part II, sections b ("The Great Man") and c ("The Advance in Intellectuality").

[37] S. Freud, *Group Psychology*, p. 74.

[38] Ibid., p. 76.

[39] Freud had translated Bernheim's *De la suggestion et de ses applications à la thérapeutique* (1886) in 1888.

[40] S. Freud, *Group Psychology*, p. 89. This passage is one of the few political confessions interspersed in Freud's writings and letters. Another, even more telling, is found in his analysis of joke-making and joke-telling as a revolution *in nuce*. There, in the revolutionary year 1905, it was said: "So long as the art of healing has not gone further in making our life safe and so long as social arrangements do no more to make it more enjoyable, so long will it be impossible to stifle the voice within us that rebels against the demands of morality. Every honest man will end by making this admission, at least to himself. [...] One must bind one's own life to that of others so closely and be able to identify oneself with others so intimately that the brevity of one's own life can be overcome; and one must not fulfil the demands of one's own needs illegitimately, but must leave them unfulfilled, because only the continuance of so many unfulfilled demands can develop the power to change the order of society. But not every personal need can be postponed in this way and transferred to other people, and there is no general and final solution of the conflict." S. Freud, *Jokes and their Relation to the Unconscious* (1905), *SE* 8, 1-247, p. 110.

[41] S. Freud, *Group Psychology*, p. 135.

[42] Ibid., p. 136f.

[43] Freud's narrative of the individualizing liberation of individuals (and isolated couples) from the spell of the mass hordes is transparent on Hegel's account of the successive generalization of freedom-consciousness in the course of world history.

[44] "There are abundant indications that being in love only made its appearance late on in the sexual relations between men and women; so that the opposition between sexual love and group ties is also a late development." (S. Freud, *Group Psychology*, p. 140).

[45] Ibid., p. 140.

[46] Ibid., p. 86f.

[47] M. Horkheimer, 'The Authoritarian State', in: *Telos. Critical Theory of the Contemporary* 15 (1973), pp. 3-20, p. 20.

[48] S. Freud, *The Future of an Illusion* (1927), *SE* 21, pp. 1-56, p. 50. In the tradition of Spinoza, Feuerbach and Heine, Freud pleaded for an anti-illusionary (i.e. are-ligious) education. "By withdrawing their expectations from the other world and concentrating all their liberated energies into their life on earth, [men] will probably succeed in achieving a state of things in which life will become tolerable for everyone and civilization no longer oppressive to anyone." (ibid.)

[49] S. Freud, *Civilization and its Discontents* (1930), *SE* 21, pp. 57-146, p. 108 f.

The Social Unconscious, Trauma and Groups: A Constellation

Earl Hopper

This chapter is an edited and expanded version of my panel presentation in *Thoughts for the Times on Groups and Masses* in which I responded to an invitation from Dr Daniela Finzi "to say something about the social unconscious, trauma, and groups, which are known to be your favorite topics".[1] Actually, in an almost meta-psychological sense these three topics are aspects of the same combined topic, although I am not yet sure what this constellation should be called. In any case, I argue that whereas in order to explain the dynamics of groups of various kinds, Sigmund Freud focused on the personalities of their leaders and in effect of their followers, he did not give sufficient attention to the dynamics of groups as such and to how they influence the "emergence" of their leaders and followers. I also argue that although many social scientists and psychoanalysts have contributed to modifications of Freud's original theory, it is important to acknowledge the specific insights of Group Analysis and Group Relations, e.g. an extended paradigm of time and space, sociogenesis, the tripartite matrix of any social system, and the development of basic assumptions in the unconscious life of people in groups.[2]

The Constellation of the Social Unconscious, Trauma and Groups

The concept of the social unconscious refers to the restraints and the constraints of the foundation and dynamic matrices of our contextual social systems of which as a consequence of repression we are unaware, and/or as a consequence of denial and disavowal we refuse to be aware. The "social unconscious" emphasizes the embeddedness of relational persons in their contextual social systems from conception onwards. However, the concept refers not only to the ways that foundational and dynamic matrices of these contextual social systems affect the development of our internal worlds, but also to the properties of these contextual matrices, which can be misleading, because we already have many words to describe the external world, such as, quite simply: "society" and "culture".

This concept of the social unconscious differs from the classical concept of the collective unconscious in Jungian Analytical Psychology with its emphasis on the cosmos, the species, and the organism. Whereas the social unconscious is central to the paradigm of classical Group Analysis, it has recently been proposed that this concept becomes part of the emerging paradigm of contemporary relational psychoanalysis more generally.[3] An appreciation of the importance of political processes and the possibilities for social change are central to these schools of thought.

The external world is internalized on the basis of disappointment that the figures on whom we depend have failed to satisfy our needs and live up to our expectations. William R. D. Fairbairn[4] realized that the motivation for building up our internal worlds is the need to gain more control of our objects, take responsibility for them, and to protect them from aggression both from other people and from ourselves.

Traumatized and traumatogenic processes must be discussed together with the social unconscious. Whereas classical psychoanalysis continues to privilege drive theory (the essence of which is the Kleinian theory of the death instinct, innate malign envy and the primacy of projection), it is possible instead to privilege "trauma", which is a function of failed dependency in a significant relationship. Thus, helplessness is at the core of the human condition, and envy is an emergent defense against the anxieties of helplessness.

The "group" is the third element of my combined topic. The "group" is often used as a token for a society, a culture, and for the "social" in general. It is also used as a token for other kinds of social formation, such as an organization or a family, etc. A group is a particular kind of social system with specific properties and parameters; although all groups are social systems, not all social systems are groups.[5]

Although human beings depend on their groups and their leaders in order to survive, and much of our work occurs in groups, we are prone within them to experience various anxieties and defenses against them. Such anxieties and defenses are manifest in various forms of unconscious regression, and, therefore, to various relational processes. As Norbert Elias has argued, in the beginning human beings appeared within a breeding group or "grouping". He insisted that the very idea of an "absolute beginning" is a fallacy rooted in aspects of culture of which we are unconscious, e.g. the first words of Genesis.[6] The boundaries of groups and the members of them are extremely porous, both in time and social space. People are saturated and permeated by their socio-cultural worlds.

The Durkeim Problem as an Insignia of the Trauma of Industrialization Processes

The intertwined nature of the social unconscious, trauma and the group can be seen in "the Durkheim problem", which I have addressed in a variety of publications.[7] Whereas the division of labor associated with industrialization produced what seemed to be an unlimited amount of wealth for a limited amount of effort, this division of labor also seemed to create what Durkheim called "abnormal" developments in the economic and political structures of industrializing societies. He was not clear whether "abnormal" meant a statistical abnormality or a social pathology, the latter implying that a society was an organism which could be ill or healthy. In any case, from time-to-time people's expectations completely outstripped their levels of achievement, creating intense anxieties, including what much later sociologists called "feelings of relative deprivation", which were likely to be expressed and enacted through various personal and collective expressions of discontent, which I have called "forms of instrumental adjustment". The Establishment feared these politicized forms of instrumental adjustment, e.g. strikes, the withdrawal of labor, low productivity, forms of insurrection, rebellion and even revolution, etc., and especially crowd formations. These developments could be explained in terms of various kinds of what today we call "social trauma", e.g. extreme economic inequality, stagflation, unemployment, new structures of corporate life, the alienation of urban living, etc. In summary, social traumas were likely to give rise to patterns of relative deprivation and politicized collective forms of instrumental adjustment, some of which were themselves likely to be traumatogenic.

The Freudian Study of Groups and Groupings

In this context Freud in *Group Psychology and the Analysis of the Ego* argued that a group is a social formation in which people have projected their super-egos and perhaps their ego-ideals into the same person, who was likely to be or to become their leader on the basis of being a shared "father figure". In other words, groups are likely to form on the basis of the collusion of the participants in them with various kinds of projections and identifications of paternal super-egos, ego-ideals and ideal-egos, i.e., in terms of the elements and the dynamics of the Oedipus complex. Of course, this hypothesis assumed the systemic restraints and constraints of patriarchy. It also assumed that all social formations could be regarded as groups.

Influenced by Freud's work, many psychologists of the late 19th and early 20th centuries began to discuss these social formations and processes in terms of the personalities of the "leaders" of them, for example, Theodor Adorno *et al* with respect to the "authoritarian personality", [8] and Hannah Arendt (1951) with respect to "totalitarianism" and the "totalitarian personality".[9][10] However, S. H. Foulkes, who was influenced by the work of social scientists in Frankfurt during the 1920's and 1930's, was one of the first psychoanalysts who argued that in order to understand totalitarian leadership of various kinds of social formations, it was necessary to focus on the social dynamics of these formations.

Foulkes founded Group Analysis as a clinical discipline. He made common cause with Patrick de Mare,[11] who was especially interested in "therapy" for groups, organizations, and societies.[12] De Maré was deeply influenced by the work of Fairbairn concerning the primacy of interpersonal relations. Foulkes and de Maré were influenced by the Eliasian idea that individuals and groups are two sides of the same proverbial coin, as are the disciplines that influenced the study of them, e.g. psychoanalysis and sociology.

John Rickman, Wilfred Bion, and later Pierre Turquet and their associates, who founded the Group Relations Movement, shared these interests.[13] Rickman was devoted to the study of the societal context of organizations and groups, and emphasized the concept of the person rather than the concept of the individual member of a group. Bion conceptualized three relational but projective defenses against psychotic anxieties, which he called "basic assumptions", i.e. Pairing, Fight/Flight, and Dependency. Turquet implied that an additional basic assumption of "Oneness" should be considered.[14] However, as Kleinian analysts, Bion and Turquet emphasized the primacy of the death instinct, projection, and envy, rather than trauma, introjection, and helplessness. In my view this prevented Bion and Turquet from fully conceptualizing a fourth basic assumption.[15]

Bion also argued that each basic assumption had a kind of magnetic attraction for people with particular personality characteristics and particular anxieties. Leaders could be understood in terms of their "valences" for a particular basic assumption. This was not unlike the earlier work of Fritz Redl on the co-creation of roles and on what he called "role suction".[16] However, derived from his work on verbal communication and his interest in drama, Foulkes referred to these processes in terms of "personification".

Incohesion: Aggregation/ Massification or (ba) I:A/M as a Fourth Basic Assumption in the Unconscious Life of Groups

As a sociologist who became a group analyst and then a psychoanalyst, I have tried to integrate these approaches of Foulkes and de Mare, on the one hand, and of Bion and Turquet, on the other. I have argued that by privileging trauma in our contemporary relational psychoanalytical and group analytical paradigm, it is possible to focus on failed dependency and the fear of annihilation rather than on innate malign envy. As an expression of and as a defense against the phenomenology of the fear of annihilation, "Incohesion: Aggregation/Massification" or (ba) I:A/M becomes the fourth basic assumption in the unconscious life of groups. An outline of my theory of Incohesion is appended to this chapter.[17]

The basic assumption of Incohesion: Aggregation/Massification can and does exist in all social systems, but is especially prominent in those that have been traumatized. Like all basic assumptions, Incohesion is a property of the tripartite matrix of any social system (including the foundation matrix of the contextual society, the dynamic matrix of the organization and/or the groups, and the personal or interpersonal matrices of the members of them), and is manifest in specific patterns of relations, normation, communication, technology, styles of thinking and feeling, and styles of aggressive feelings and aggression.[18]

With respect to societies, fundamentalism is often associated with nationalism, fascism and totalitarianism, e.g. as seen in Germany, Italy, and Japan following World War I.[19] [20]Totalitarianism in Czechoslovakia has been discussed by Klimova.[21] Such societies can be understood as traumatized. However, in accordance with the basic message of "Judgment at Nuremberg" (1961), such societies must also be understood in the context of a global social system, the study of which continues to be neglected. Several current but less extreme examples of traumatized societies and their totalitarian leadership include the United States and Trump, the United Kingdom and Johnson, Italy and Berlusconi and Meloni, Russia and Putin, etc. These so-called "leaders" are personifiers of the processes of Incohesion that are typical of their societies. I have argued that assassination of political leaders can be understood in this context.[22]

With respect to organizations, fundamentalism is often associated with fanaticism.[23] I have experienced fanatical intolerance during the Kleinian ascendency in the Institute of Psychoanalysis in London. This involved expressions of contempt towards analysts who did not accept Kleinian assumptions, and the marginalization of those who were in more open disagreement with them. These processes were led by a defensive Kleinian "matriarchy", perhaps following a flawed Freudian "patriarchy". [24] It was in this context that Bollas and I began to elucidate the fascist state of mind. I would argue that these developments have led to the collapse of the hegemony of psychoanalysis in England.

More recently, I have seen intolerant scapegoating at the Tavistock and Portman NHS Foundation Trust with respect to the ways in which gender identity disorders were treated.[25] Anyone who questioned whether it was appropriate to give puberty blockers to young children, at least before they were able to participate in some kinds of exploration of family and personal dynamics, were exposed to the violence of silence combined with the tearful distress of the leaders of this approach. I have experienced intolerant scapegoating in the American Group Psychotherapy Association in which those who challenged the dilution of the clinical project in the context of political wokeness were regarded as racially prejudiced.[26] The Group Analytic Society International and many of the Institutes of Group Analysis associated with it have begun to fetishize, ritualize and concretize the theory and concepts of the social unconscious and of intersectionality. Social demography is used as a substitute for processes of sociogenesis, interpersonal relationality, and personification. This has led to the neglect of personal/interpersonal matrices, which are the crucible of individuality, personal responsibility, and creativity.[27] As a consequence, colleagues who continue to identify with more traditional models of psychopathology and clinical work in groups have been increasingly relegated.[28]

Such professional organizations struggle with the aftermath of various trauma, some of which are typical of the mental health field.[29] They have suffered from "stress" trauma associated with over-expansion and competition for scarce resources. They have also suffered a loss of status, partly associated with their membership becoming mostly female and non-medical. Some of these problems are associated with a shift from clinical work in private practice to clinical work in public institutions. The development of drug treatments for an increased variety of affective disorders has also been a factor in the threats to identity of the members of mental health professions. In addition to the effects of these "cumulative" trauma, such organizations have also suffered "cataclysmic" trauma associated with boundary breaking by senior, highly regarded members of our profession, leading to profound disappointment and the need to de-idealize the clinical process and the leadership of these core organizations.[30] Such boundary breaking is in itself both a consequence of these traumatogenic processes and a source of further trauma. Character assassination can be understood in the context of the processes of aggression that are typical of these organizations.[31]

How Might Group Analysis be of Help?

Durkheim thought that the Guilds of various occupations and professions might help a society manage the anomogenic processes that followed from social trauma. However, the rivalry and hatred within the foundation matrices of their contextual societies were repeated and enacted within the dynamic matrices of these organizations. It is hardly surprising that the Guilds were prone to the dynamics of Incohesion, including the totalitarian leadership of them.

Although we have learned a great deal about the personalities of those who become leaders of various kinds of crowds, groups, organizations, and societies, we have had comparatively few studies of their leadership processes.[32] Despite their calls for studies of leadership as such, group analysts have very rarely produced them, with notable exceptions.[33] We still know less about leadership than we do about leaders.[34]

In her S.H. Foulkes Lecture Regine Scholz (2022) expressed her conviction that work with constructed large groups is more important than ever. She acknowledged the early work of de Mare and his students who argued that participation in large groups would lead to koinonia or interpersonal fellowship, based on increased insight as well as increased "outsight", which would, in turn, lead to greater rationality and cooperation. This was analogous to Freud's hope that on the basis of psychoanalytical experience "Where id was, there shall ego be".[35] Other forms of collective self-reflection are also important, e.g., social dreaming matrices,[36] social dream telling,[37] the reflective citizens movement,[38] and trilogy events.[39] These projects draw on psychoanalytical theories of collective regression.

Conclusion

The psychoanalytical study of various kinds of social formation, including groups and groupings, such as hordes and masses, as well as committees, organizations, and their contextual societies, is both deeper and wider than the study of the personalities of their leaders. Psychoanalysis itself, both pure and applied, and both clinical and empirical, has become much more complex since its conception in terms of trauma as a violation of the safety shield, let alone the possibility that trauma was a matter of the regulation of Oedipal phantasies. Long before the death of Freud, it had become clear that although unconscious processes were rooted in the species and in the body, unconscious processes were also a function of social, cultural, and political processes, or in other words of both Psyche and her social world. This was not merely a matter of distinguishing fantasy from phantasy, but of extending our very notion of the individual human being from the organism to the "person-in-relationship-with others" within a transgenerational context. It must be acknowledged that although much of this is implied in Freud's work, it is usually made explicit only in response to polemics against Freud's and his colleagues' attempts to formulate a biology of the mind. No matter how much we appreciate this shift from the study of persons in the context of philosophy and religion in their most narrow sense, it is essential to bring into focus the dynamics of the external social world. The sociology of the mind augments the biology of the mind.

If it is true that by the group we have been formed, it is also true that through the study of the group we can develop a more comprehensive understanding of ourselves, both individually and collectively. And if is true that by the group we have been harmed, it is also true that by the group we can be healed. At least in part. Such healing processes require an appreciation of the complexity and power of social processes of which we are unconscious, especially those associated with transgenerational social trauma, which we have also co-created. The study of basic assumption processes and their personifications is of universal and eternal importance. I am hopeful that with insight into the dynamics of Incohesion we can at least mitigate the repetition of them. It is necessary to regain the ability and willingness to exercise the transcendent imagination, and stop the repetition of trauma and revenge.

Thank you for this opportunity to express a few of my "thoughts for the times on groups and masses." We have much to celebrate, but also have much work to do.

Appendix
An Outline of my Theory of the Basic Assumption of Incohesion:
Aggregation/Massification

1. *Traumatic Experience*

   - Various events that are experienced in terms of inadequate containment and insufficient holding can be characterized in terms of the failed dependency of oppression, stress, accumulative, and/or catastrophic personal and/or social trauma.
   - Social trauma involves large numbers of people, more or less at the same time, e.g. war, famine, changes in employment structures, rates of inequality, political failures, Brexit, or even the Covid "syndemic".

2. *Personal Dynamics*

   Traumatic events are likely to cause:

   - the fear of annihilation, i.e. that our lives and our psychic lives are in danger, our safety shields have failed us, and we might be obliterated existentially; this fear is characterized by intra-psychic fission and fragmentation, and various psychotic anxieties associated with this, in oscillation with relational fusion and confusion with what is left of, and with what can be found in, the other, and various psychotic anxieties associated with these polarities (falling apart, feeling in bits and pieces, suffocating, drowning, falling for ever, petrification, etc);
   - envy of those who might be of help but who refuse to do so;
   - the development of negative and positive encapsulations, encystments, and/or encrypments;
   - the development of crustacean and amoeboid character structures;
   - the propensity to enact aggressive and violent feelings in aggression and violence;
   - traumatophilia involving evacuation of intolerable feelings, sadism, attempts to control the object, attempts to turn passive into active, and the repetition of trauma in the service of communication;
   - the trauma/addiction syndrome involving somatization, sado-masochistic sexuality, substance abuse, risk taking, delinquency and criminality.

3. *Social System Dynamics*

- In the context of these traumatogenic processes, social systems of various kinds are likely to regress and to become groups or group-like in their structures; as such they are likely to become characterized by the dynamics of basic assumptions.
- The basic assumption of Incohesion is a manifestation of the intra-psychic phenomenology of the fear of annihilation and relational forms of defensive protection against the pain of this experience, as seen in the primary development within the social system of the socio-cultural state of aggregation, in the secondary development of the socio-cultural state of massification, and then in the defensive oscillations between them;
- Incohesion is associated with the development of social psychic retreats, such as ghettos and enclaves, which are often based on sub-groupings and contra-groupings associated with social identities;
- All basic assumptions within the foundation matrix of a society are likely to be manifest in the dynamic matrices of their constitutive groupings, and, thus, the constitutive groupings of a society characterized by Incohesion are themselves likely to be characterized by Incohesion.

4. *Personification and Role Suction*

- All basic assumptions are characterized by the co-creation of roles that are typical of them;
- Such roles have a high degree of suction power;
- People vary in their vulnerability to the suction power of particular roles or to their valences for such roles;
- As a consequence of their traumatophilia and their trauma/addiction syndromes, traumatized people are especially vulnerable to the suction power of the roles that are typical of Incohesion, and, in turn, are likely to personify them, as seen in those people with authoritarian, totalitarian, absolutist personalities, etc.
- Some of the roles that are typical of Incohesion can be considered in terms of aggregation, and others in terms of massification.

5. Transgenerational Incohesion

- Traumatized people are likely to perpetuate traumatic experience, and, thus, they are likely to perpetuate Incohesion;
- Incohesion is likely to be transgenerational.

6. The twin pillars of massification as a defence against aggregation as a consequence of social trauma and the fear of annihilation, are two-fold: fundamentalism and scapegoating

- Closely associated with patriarchy, fundamentalism involves a continuing sacralization of core beliefs, values and activities, and is associated with social category thinking and feeling.
- The purity of fundamentalism involves processes of scapegoating through which individual people, groupings and ideas who stand up against the group-as-a-whole are peripheralized, marginalized and excluded, as well as sacrificed.
- Fundamentalism and scapegoating lead to and are associated with totalitarianism, fascism, and fanaticism.

Notes

1   As seen in, for example, E. Hopper, *The Social Unconscious: Selected Papers.* London: Jessica Kingsley Publishers, 2003; E. Hopper, *Traumatic Experience in the Unconscious Life of Groups.* London: Jessica Kingsley Publishers, 2003; E. Hopper. & H. Weinberg (Eds.), *The Social Unconscious in Persons, Groups and Societies:* Vol. 1 (*Mainly Theory*), Vol. 2 (*Mainly Matrices*) and Vol. 3 (*The Foundation Matrix Extended and re-Configured*). London: Karnac, 2011, 2016 and 2017.
2   I have cited many of my own publications, which I regard as forgivable, because they have extensive references to the relevant work of others.
3   J. Tubert-Oklander, 'Beyond Psychoanalysis and Group Analysis: The Urgent Need for a New Paradigm of the Human Being', in: *Group Analysis* 52/4 (2019), pp. 409-426; E. Hopper, '"Notes" for My Response to the Foulkes Lecture by Juan Tubert-Oklander, May 2019', in: *Group Analysis* 52/4 (2019), pp. 427-433.
4   W. R. Fairbairn, *Psycho-Analytic Studies of the Personality.* London: Tavistock Publications, 1952.
5   E. Hopper, 'A Sociological View of Large Groups', in: L. Kreeger (Ed.), *The Large Group: Dynamics and Therapy.* London: Constable, 1975. Reprinted in 2003 in *The Social Unconscious: Selected Papers.* London: Jessica Kingsley Publishers. H. Foulkes, *Introduction to Group Analytic Psychotherapy.* London: Karnac, 1983 [1948].

[6] N. Elias, *The Civilising Process*. Oxford: Blackwell, 1938.

[7] E.g. E. Hopper, *Social Mobility: A Study of Social Control and Insatiability*. Oxford: Blackwell, 1981; E. Hopper, 'Imagination and Hope in Relational and Group Analytic Perspectives', in: *Group Analytic – Contexts* 85 (2019). https://groupanalyticsociety.co.uk/contexts/issue-85/articles/hope-and-group-analysis/3-imagination-and-hope-in-relational-and-group-analytic-perspectives/ (accessed 30-07-2024).

[8] T. W. Adorno, E. Frenkel-Brunswik, D. Levinson & R. Sanford, *The Authoritarian Personality*. New York: Harper Brothers, 1950. Colleagues today are less familiar with the work of Edward Shils who stressed that the structure of the authoritarian personality was independent of political beliefs and ideology; there was authoritarianism of the Left as well as of the Right (E. Shils, *The Torment of Secrecy: The Background and Consequences of American Security Policies*. Glencoe, Ill: Free Press, 1956).

[9] H. Arendt, *The Origins of Totalitarianism*. Berlin: Schocken Books, 1951.

[10] Many other versions of these personality and character types have been adumbrated. Heinz Kohut (*The Restoration of the Self*. New York: Int. Univ. Press, 1977) distinguished benign from malignant forms of narcissism, and Otto Kernberg ('Leadership and Organizational Functioning: Organizational Regression', in: *International Journal of Group Psychotherapy* 28/1 (1978), pp. 3-25) in his comprehensive theories of malignant narcissism referred to Serge Moscovici's (Notes towards a Description of Social Representations, in: *European Journal of Social Psychology* 18 (1988), pp. 211-250) analysis of "the merchant of illusions". Christopher Bollas ('The Fascist State of Mind', in: *Being a Character*. London: Routledge, 1992) and I described the "fascist state of mind" (E. Hopper, 'Aggregation/Massification and Fission (Fragmentation)/Fusion: A Fourth Basic Assumption', paper presented to the VIII International Conference of the IAGP, Amsterdam, 1989; E. Hopper, 'Notes on Psychotic Anxieties and Society: Fission (Fragmentation)/Fusion and Aggregation/Massification', paper for the Conference of the Royal College of Psychiatry, Cambridge, UK, 1989). Janine Chasseguet-Smirgel (*Creativity and Perversion*. London: Free Association Books, 1985) emphasized perverse character structures. Vamik Volkan and his colleagues (*On the Spectrum of Narcissism: A Clinical Study of Healthy Narcissism*. Gottingen: Vandenhoeck & Ruprecht,1994) distinguished reparative from destructive forms of narcissistic and charismatic leadership. Michael Sebek ('The Fate of the Totalitarian Object', in: *International Forum of Psychoanalysis* 5/4, pp. 289-294 (1996) discussed the "totalitarian object". Sverre Varin ('Fundamentalist Mindset', in: *The Scandinavian Psychoanalytic Review* 40/2, pp. 94-104) has outlined the "fundamentalist mindset", and Karl Figlio ('Psychoanalysis, Reparation and Historical Memory', in: *American Imago* 71/4 (2014), pp. 417-443) has referred to the "absolutist personality".

[11] P. de Mare, *Perspectives in Group Psychotherapy*. London: Allen & Unwin, 1972.

[12] E. Hopper, 'From Objects and Subjects to Citizens: Group Analysis and the Study of Maturity', in: *Group Analysis* 33/1 (2000), pp. 29-34.

[13] J. Rickman, *No Ordinary Psychoanalyst: The Exceptional Contributions of John Rickman*, P. King (Ed.). London: Karnac, 2003; W. R. Bion, *Experiences in Groups and Other Papers*. London: Tavistock Publications, 1961.

[14] P. Turquet, 'Threats to Identity in the Large Group', in: L. Kreeger (Ed.), *The Large Group: Dynamics and Therapy*. London: Constable, 1975. Reprinted in 1994 in London by Karnac.

[15] This was also true for Lionel Kreeger (see fn. above) who, it is often overlooked, edited Turquet's famous chapter in *The Large Group* from Turquet's rather rough notes.

[16] F. Redl, 'Group Emotion and Leadership', in: *Psychiatry* 5 (1942), pp. 573-596.

[17] E. Hopper, *The Social Unconscious: Selected Papers*. London: Jessica Kingsley Publishers, 2003; E. Hopper, '"Notes" on the Theory and Concept of the Fourth Basic Assumption in the Unconscious Life of Groups and Group-like Social Systems: Incohesion: Aggregation/Massification or (ba) I:A/M', in: C. Penna (Ed.), *From Crowd Psychology to the Dynamics of Large Groups: Historical, Theoretical and Practical Considerations*. London: Routledge, 2023, pp. 179-195.

[18] E. Hopper, 'The Tripartite Matrix in Foulkesian Group Analysis', in: Id. (Ed.) *The Tripartite Matrix in the Developing Theory and Expanding Practice of Group Analysis: The Social Unconscious in Persons, Groups and Societies: Vol. 4*. London: Routledge, 2024, pp. 35-43.

[19] E. Hopper, 'Intolerance and Processes of Fundamentalism in the Context of the Basic Assumption of Incohesion: Aggregation/Massification: Theoretical Notes and Clinical Illustrations', in: A. Berman & G. Ofer (Eds.), *Tolerance – A Concept in Crisis: Psychoanalytic, Group Analytic and Socio-Cultural Perspectives*. London: Routledge, 2024, pp. 160-171. L. Auestad, *Psychoanalysis and Politics: Exclusion and the Politics of Representation*. London: Karnac, 2012.

[20] I often think that the best examples of totalitarian leaders and leadership dynamics are found in Shakespeare's *Julius Caesar*, and in the famous film *Viva Zapata*. Caesar and Zapata were massification leaders, and Cassius and the "Trotsky" were aggregation leaders, or personifyers of massification and aggregation processes respectively.

[21] H. Klimová, 'The False We/the False Collective Self: A Dynamic Part of the Social Unconscious', in: E. Hopper. & H. Weinberg (Eds.), *The Social Unconscious in Persons, Groups and Societies:* Vol. 1 (*Mainly Theory*), London: Karnac, 2011, pp. 187-208.

[22] E. Hopper, *Traumatic Experience in the Unconscious Life of Groups*. London: Jessica Kingsley Publishers, 2003.

[23] E. Hopper, 'Intolerance and Processes of Fundamentalism' (see fn. 19).

[24] As early as 1961, Erving Goffman referred to "total institutions", and argued that they were prone to totalitarian leadership. Such processes are exemplified in the novel by Ken Kesly (1962) and the film *One Flew Over the Cuckoo's Nest*.

[25] H. Barnes, *Time to Think: The Inside Story of the Collapse of the Tavistock's Gender Service for Children*. London: Swift Press, 2023; D. Bell, 'First Do No Harm', in: *International Journal of Psychoanalysis* 101/5 (2020), pp. 1031-1038.

26 E. Hopper, 'Processes of Scapegoating and Sibling Rivalry in the Context of the Basic Assumption of Incohesion: Aggregation/Massification Or (ba) I:A/M', in: S. Ashuach & A. Berman (Eds.), *Sibling Relations and the Horizontal Axis in Theory and Practice. Contemporary Group Analysis, Psychoanalysis and Organization Consultancy*. London: Routledge, 2022, pp. 132-145.

27 E. Hopper, '"Notes" on the Theory and Concept'.

28 L. Bronshtein, 'My Experience of Group Therapy Training at an Ideologically Captured Institution', in: *Critical Therapy Antidote*, May 2024. https://criticaltherapyantidote.org/2024/05/24/my-experience-of-group-therapy-training-at-an-ideologically-captured-institution (accessed 30-07-2024).

29 E. Hopper (Ed.), *Trauma and Organisations*. London: Karnac, 2012.

30 W. Godley, 'Saving Masud Khan', in: *London Review of Books* 22 (2018), pp. 3-7. J. Hook, 'Sexual Boundary Violations: Victims, Perpetrators and Risk Reduction', in: *BJPsych Advances* 24 (2018), pp. 374-383.

31 E. Hopper, *Traumatic Experience in the Unconscious Life of Groups*. London: Jessica Kingsley Publishers, 2003.

32 This is not to overlook that in the context of American social psychology, sociology more generally, and political science, there have been many studies of what is often called "collective behavior", for example, the classic text entitled *Collective Behaviour* by Ralph H. Turner and Lewis M. Killian, Englewood Cliffs, NJ: Prentice-Hall, 1957.

33 E. g. R. Stacey, 'The Science of Complexity: An Alternative Perspective for Strategic Change Processes', in: *Strategic Management Journal* 16/6 (1995), pp. 477-495; G. Binney, P. Glanfield & G. Wilke, *Breaking Free of Bonkers: How to Lead in Today's Crazy World of Organizations*. London: Hachette, 2017; C. Thornton (Ed.), *The Art and Science of Working Together: Practising Group Analysis in Teams and Organisations*. London: Routledge, 2019.

34 M. Maccoby & M. Cortina (Eds.), *Leadership, Psychoanalysis and Society*. London: Routledge, 2022; V. D. Volkan, S. Akhtar, R. M. Dorn, J. S. Kafka, O. Kernberg, P. Olsson, R. Rogers. & S. Shanfield, 'Leaders and Decision-Making', in: *Mind and Human Interaction* 9 (1998), pp. 130-181

35 S. Freud, *New Introductory Lectures On Psycho-Analysis* (1933), SE 22, pp. 1-182, p. 80. – Scholz also acknowledged the seminal work of Lionel Kreeger (*The Large Group*. London: Routledge, 1975) and Stanley Schneider & Haim Weinberg (Eds., *The Large Group Revisited: The Herd, Primal Horde, Crowds and Masses*. London: Jessica Kingsley, 2003), and in effect the work of those who contributed to these volumes to which I would add the work of Josef Shaked and the subsequent work of Gerhard Wilke (*The Art of Group Analysis in Organisations*. London: Karnac 2014), Carla Penna (ed.), *From Crowd Psychology to the Dynamics of Large Groups: Historical, Theoretical and Practical Considerations*. London: Routledge, 2023) and myself, e.g., 'Convening a Large Group in Group Analysis: Two Core Principles', in: *Contexts* 98 (2022).

36 W. G. Lawrence, *Tongued with Fire: Groups in Experience*. London: Karnac, 2000.

[37] R. Friedman, *Dream-telling, Relations, and Large Groups.* London: Routledge, 2019.

[38] M. Mojovic, 'Totalitarian and Post-Totalitarian Matrices: Reflective Citizens Facing Social-Psychic Retreats', in: B. Huppertz (Ed.), *Approaches to Psychic Trauma: Theory and Practice.* New York & London: Rowman & Littlefield, 2019, pp. 159-177).

[39] R. Morgan-Jones, 'The trilogy matrix event (TME): A Setting for Collective Reflection on Social System Dynamics of the Tripartite Matrix', in: E. Hopper (Ed.), T*he Tripartite Matrix in the Developing Theory and Expanding Practice of Group Analysis: The Social Unconscious in Persons, Groups and Societies: Vol. 4.* London: Routledge, 2024, pp. 247-261.

The In-Between of Us:
The Inter-Subject and Interstitial Belonging

Francisco J. González

Being Singular Plural

To be human is to belong. Freud noted the helplessness of the infant, helpless to the point of utter dependence on external care for its existence, which Winnicott would develop into the famous slogan of his radically intersubjectivist credo: there is no baby without a mother. Today we can confidently extend that psychoanalytic tenet to say that *neither is there a subject without a group.* The lifelong layering of belonging constitutes an essential part of human subjectivity – belonging in nested, expanding, intersecting, overlapping, conflicting and conflictual groups. The complex terrain of such belonging opens, in fact, from the very start: for a baby is never simply in relation to one caregiving other, but to a network of relations, complexly organized. The rosy bubble of early maternal preoccupation is not a hermetically sealed enclosure; it is porous, intersected by a variety of others. To the extent that it occurs, it does because it is made possible through connection with others.

In earlier writings[1] I describe what I have variously called "the collective of the individual", "one-to-many object relations", or "groupal objects." These designations attempt to elaborate a specific theoretical link between individual subjectivity and the collective. Mainstream psychoanalytic theory has been decidedly individualist in its theoretical orientation, despite the turn in late Freudian texts which could have opened onto a much needed extension of theory premised on a different register: the collective. But rather than make use of this opening, and for reasons that have everything to do with group formation (keeping *us* cohered by keeping *them* out), organizational psychoanalysis has largely expelled the teachings of group analysis and dissociated itself from its implications.[2] This is no longer tenable.

Francisco J. González

In an accelerating world compacted by technology, intensifying frictions between groups generate enormous psychic heat, at levels both singular and collective. Increasingly, individual patients seek help for the conditions born of the discontents of group life: some for matters pertaining to identity (whether incoherent and diffused, rigidified, misrecognized, or fractured); some feeling radically disconnected, alienated, haunted by a sense of displacement and exile in lives which lack belonging; some for the damage done by the traumas of oppression, driven by xenophobic hatreds in the first person plural (racisms of various kinds, misogyny, homo- and trans-phobias)[3]; many for the ill-defined anxiety of living in a world going mad, overwhelmed by the tsunami of History, engulfed by the helplessness of individuality in the face of problems which can only be attended to effectively by collectives. In short, if for Freud hysteria was the privileged site of the psychoanalytic elaboration, for us it may well be the group. The climate crisis, war and its refugees, racism and xenophobia, economic disparities, political cataclysm and the dangerous fascistic tendencies emerging from democratic instabilities – all challenge the stability and creative growth not only of communities but also of the individuals comprising them. And further: these matters raise important theoretical questions about the nature, place, and practice of psychoanalysis.

Collectivization can be understood as occurring under the sign of the social unconscious which should be differentiated from the repressed, dynamic unconscious familiar to any psychoanalyst.[4] The latter is the domain of the individual. Even in contemporary theories which have elevated the importance of intersubjectivity, theorization returns to the effects or the inscription of the other (most conventionally figured as the maternal object) within the individual psyche. But the social unconscious – while having profound effects on the unconscious structuring of individuals – can best be understood as emanating from a wholly different register. Staying for a moment with the individual, while paraphrasing and extending Freud's famous definition of the drive ("Trieb"): if the personal unconscious results from the effects of the demand placed on the mind for work in consequence of its relationship to the body, the social unconscious can be understood as the demand placed on the mind for work in consequence of its relationship to the group. The operations of this dimension of the unconscious for the individual, then, concern its collective aspects, and can best be understood through a history of what could loosely be called *group* object relationships.

But what does it mean, psychoanalytically, to be a member of a group.

The group theorist Rene Käes advances the idea that to belong to a group means precisely this: to be subject to these kinds of unconscious pacts and alliances.[5] Subjectivity has here a dual face: yes, the location for the elaboration of individual psyche and its vibrant (though always limited) agency, but also the site of subjection, a kind of submission to the unconscious structuring of the group. Seen from this angle, the notion of belonging cannot be reduced in a facile way to a comforting and friendly accommodation – though the experience of membership in a collective is constitutive of the warm embrace of what we often fondly call "humane", and its correlate "humanity". Belonging in this psychoanalytic sense is less idealized; it has a cost and a burden. The group makes a claim on us in our belonging to it, it has us in its purchase in some way, it owns something of us.

The alliances Kaës speaks of are the collective repressions, fantasies, norms, taboos and dreams, the transmitted mythological traumas and glories (as Volkan[6] might say) that define that group. By way of loose description, these might take the form of lemmas: *Boys don't cry. In this family we stick together no matter what. America is the land of opportunity. Psychoanalysis is dyadic. Etc...*

The story is much more complex, however. This model of collective identification must be extended to all manner of other markers of who we think ourselves to be, along the lines of gender, geography, nationality, class, religious, ethnic and racialized difference, and so forth. The foundational and dynamic matrices of groups and social organizations thus constitute vital collective aspects of our individual subjectivity, the layering of one-to-many object relationships building up corresponding psychic structures that are not individual but groupal – more like a "we-ego".[7] We "boys" – we "children" – we "dark-skinned ones" – we "who speak Pashtun, Hebrew, English, Swahil", and so forth. And these collective psychic structures are as robust and emotionally significant as those stemming from individual object ties.

If we consider the subject from a perspective that includes this collective dimension, we can conclude with Käes that the subject is thus most properly an "intersubject":

> divided between the demands imposed on him by the necessity of serving his own purposes and those that derive from his status and function as a member of an intersubjective chain [that is, as a member of a group with its particular history], of which he is at one and the same time the servant, the link of transmission, the heir, and the actor.[8]

Postulating the group as a fundamental organizer of the psyche on par with individual objects, leads to the logical conclusion that the unconscious has a dual origin: if the organismal body provides a kind of floor for the individual unconscious, groups and social organizations and their histories (which are necessary conditions for the survival of that organismal body), provide something like its ceiling in the social unconscious.

Human subjectivity properly speaking is then that subjectivity operating precisely at the intersection between these two domains of the body and the group – each with its different orders of materiality and temporality. Like the dual theory of light in physics, the human subject is both particle and wave. This inherent double inscription is further complicated by the multiplicity of group memberships. No individual is a member of only one group, and all groups are pluralities, encompassing significant differences. When I speak of this double provenance of the unconscious, I do not mean that the *individual* must find its relationship to the group, accept or resist its domination, strive for its individuation, etc. I mean more radically that the subject *is* inherently and always liminal – its location is always at a frontier, border, or boundary between the (subhuman) limit of the body and the (superhuman) limit of group histories. The subject is the interference pattern that forms between two waves: like the arrangement of ripples on the surface of a pond when two stones are thrown closely together. One stone is the body, one is the group. From this perspective, there is no such thing as an "individual" subjectivity – because the psyche is never indivisible, never simply closed in on, fully distinct or differentiated, or "contained" within itself, even for the mythic being who is completely analyzed and at the zenith of a fully realized depressive position. Each subjectivity is always and already deeply divided by the myriad of collectives necessarily criss-crossing its existence.

We could speak instead of *singular* subjectivities, the singular locations of those interference patterns, the density of histories that build up like a meshwork of intersecting threads, the accumulated interference patters that come of our border existence between a "unit status" life in this particular body (according to Winnicott) and the many memberships in groups that transmit their histories through us, as we form the living links of those intersubjective chains (according to Käes).

The philosopher Jean-Luc Nancy describes this as *being singular plural*, and develops a whole ontology based upon it. In his essay "The Inoperative Community," he describes the "singular being, which is not the individual, [but] is the finite being."[9] To develop the contrast: an *individual* develops, detaches, or proceeds *from* something, a background or matrix; we speak, famously, of a "process of individuation." But *singularity* does not develop from or out of something, it "is made up only of the network, the interweaving, and the sharing of singularities."

Nancy radically shifts the plane of understanding away from the individual psyche, while at the same time opposing the idea of a mystically unified group mind. There is no original and unified community that we have lost, he says. The search for communal sovereignty, for a kind of Eden of the perfectly unified group, is what one sees in unreconstructed nationalisms, cult thinking, fundamentalisms, or supremacist collectives seeking the restoration of idealized lost communities. Instead, Nancy offers us a vision of a kind of being which is radically *being-with*, in which our singularity is only possible by and through our plurality, our co-being with the singular beings of others, who are the "same" in also being singular but by so being are also then always necessarily "other" in their singularity.

I bring us to this philosophical digression for three reasons:
1. Nancy provides an ontological basis for what I call the necessity of belonging to groups. He specifies that being is only ever being-with. With Nancy we can assert that belonging to a collective is not just important; it is, in fact, the necessary condition of our being in the first place.
2. The domain of being is an increasingly important one for our discipline. Increasingly psychoanalysis is moving from a practice which emphasizes ways of *knowing* to one which emphasizes ways of *being* – the facilitation of experience, cultivation of states of aliveness. That is, we are moving from a psychoanalytic *epistemology* to a psychoanalytic *ontology* as Thomas Ogden has recently written.[10]
3. This ontological realm of being, bodies, and experience brings us to a consideration of materiality in psychoanalysis. An area we have neglected in what I call our "upward bias" towards the important (and necessary) but over-valued (and never sufficient) goal of representation. In addition to understanding processes of representation we must consider processes of presentation and of incarnation, of what Bataille has called the "unleashing of passions."

This nodal subjectivity which I am trying to describe, which is located at the cross-roads between the life of the body and the life of the group, which exists as both particle and wave, this *being singular plural*, means there are enormous centrifugal forces at work in our psyches.

No group is ever completely unified, even under the banner of a chosen trauma. All groups are pluralities, with manifold positions. All groups

Francisco J. González

experience a tension between the forces of binding coherence and those of dispersing multiplicity. There is never only one way to be Austrian, "American", black, a man, bisexual, a vegetarian, Spanish-speaking, a psychoanalyst, etc. And so any group – be it of vegetarians or psychoanalysts – will find division and diversity in its ranks, and this sectioning will place traction on both the group and the singular subject. Likewise, every individual is a member of multiple groups. All subjects are intersectional, all are multiply inflected by the variety of groups that make up aspects of identity.

And so... the intersubject – sectioned and intersected, "intersectional" (to extend on the work of legal scholar Kimberlé Crenshaw) – is one subjected to enormous centrifugal forces: *pulled out* of itself into diverse memberships by the groups which grant its being, while being *pulled apart* in their multiplicity.[11] Bromberg's famous relational dictum — that health in the individual requires "standing in the spaces" of different object-relational configurations – is not only a matter of individual subjectivity, then, for the singular subject must stand in the interstitial spaces, at the borders and intersections of group belonging.[12]

Group Matter

To be an intersubject, then, is to be subject to the complex history of groups, to the social unconscious of alliances, pacts, repressions, and ideologies, many of which are undergirded by inequities of power, which are passed into us and lived through us by our memberships in them.

But the categories of identity – nationality, class, ethnicity, religion, racialized difference, gender, occupation, sexuality, regional and political affiliation, and so forth (already the proliferation of categories threatens the coherence of selfsameness) – are themselves, at the level of the psyche, nothing other than the complex history of belonging and of exile from a series of specific groups.

These groups are no more abstract than a mother is abstract. My nationality or gender is built on group object relationships comprised of lived experience, as complex and lively as my maternal object relationship. And these groups – the small collectives of everyday life – are highly contingent, attaining existence only in certain material iterations, in particular places. The innumerable repeated meals at the family table, the daily attendance at school, the annual analytic conference – groups take form in the rhythms of presence and absence.

70

It is here that the work of the Argentinian individual and group analyst Enrique Pichon-Rivière is so useful.[13] His concept of *vínculo* is that of a living link connecting the external group with the internal group of fantasy. The *vínculo* bridges internal and external. For Pichon-Rivière, the singular subject itself is already a group: one which is endlessly re-made in a "dialectical spiral" of what Klein would have called introjection and projection, as internal psychic groups and their external materializations re-create and reconstruct themselves continuously over time:

> [...] all unconscious life, that is to say, the domain of unconscious fantasy, should be considered as an interaction between internal objects (the internal group) in a permanent dialectical interrelationship with the objects of the external world.[14]

The image of the spiral brings temporality to bear on the movements of our involvement in groups. Our interaction with these memberships is dynamic: to belong in a group is a matter of subjection, yes, but also of modification and adaptability, processes which implicate the temporal. At its best, our membership in a multiplicity of groups allows creative growth, both of ourselves (our internal groups) and of the groups to which we belong (external groups). External groups alter the domain of our unconscious fantasy, as we become subject to the histories they inscribe within us, while the internal groups we project onto them may help inflect and shape the unconscious alliances and dreams of the groups to which we belong.

Aggressivity

Isolation, we know, breeds violence. The dog kept caged and sequestered will attack when exposed to others. Its cure is relatedness. Belonging is the necessary condition of relatedness and what makes us human; it is the the bedrock of civilization, which is just another word for creative collectivization. In *Civilization and its Discontents*, Freud asserts that

> [h]uman life in common is only made possible when a majority comes together which is stronger than any separate individual. [...] This re-placement of the power of the individual by the power of a community constitutes the decisive step of civilization.[15]

But as we have seen, belonging to a group also exposes the ego to its inherent divisions — to the impossibility of its individuality, to the centrifugal forces that threaten its ontological coherence. Profound experiences of belonging simultaneously expose the seams of our being, placing us in relationships that are "outside" of ourselves.

Too often the counter to the centrifugal force of potential dissolution is enforced cohesion. Both egos and groups establish and maintain – and at times police – a boundary demarcating inside from out. The relative stability of such demarcations allows secure-enough shelter for more liquid processes within. The cell wall, the skin, the doorway, the border – all are sites of enormous activity. Interaction and exchange with the world is a necessary condition of vitality; metabolism, like breathing, requires transport across these thresholds. Too porous, and liquid processes leak out diminishing the organism; not permeable enough, and the organism suffocates.

Modernity, according to the sociologist and philosopher Zygmunt Bauman, has been obsessed with making order, patrolling the limits of the group (its inevitable counterpart is therefore chaos). "Power", he writes, "is a fight against ambivalence. Fear of ambivalence is born of power: it is the power's horror (premonition?) of defeat."[16] It is precisely here that Bauman refers to the imperative of the Freudian project, celebrating the *contingency* of interpretation and its capacity to open the plurality and indeterminacy of meaning as a guard against the cruelties of power. "Ambivalence is not to be bewailed. It is to be celebrated. Ambivalence is the limit to the power of the powerful. For the same reason, it is the freedom of the powerless."[17] Ambivalence threatens the clean lines of categorized order. This was always the site of action for Freud – as far back as his theory of the erogenous zones – always the frontier, the border, the preeminent location of ambivalence.

In the modernist world where Freud began his thinking, it was perhaps sufficient to keep to the ambivalences of the "individual," and allow the group to remain in the background of the analytic field. But I would venture that despite their seeming incongruity, it is no mere coincidence that *Group Psychology and the Analysis of the Ego* appears just a year after *Beyond the Pleasure Principle*, with its introduction of the death drive in the aftermath of "the terrible war."[18] Indeed, the problems that preoccupy Freud in his late texts are the problems of "civilization", which have greatly to do with relations between and within groups. If the two world wars install for the first time in human history a global consciousness, managing ambivalence at the level of the group has become perhaps our most pressing collective problem.[19] As the world becomes ever smaller, intergroup tensions escalate, and ambivalence breeds existential anxiety. Because we are intersubjects whose sense of coherence depends not only on good-enough individual object relations but on our relations of belonging, hegemonic power can supply the illusion of psychological solidity through the violent imposition of order.

But the delusion of ordered coherence is no match for the complexities of being. In his book *Identity and Violence*, the Nobel prize winning economist Amartya Sen, emphasizes the inescapable plurality of identity and argues that violence can only be promoted by its simplification – it is a failure to recognize that "we are *diversely different*" both by membership in multiple groups and by the differences within any such grouping.[20] The reductionism of enforced cohesions serves tyranny at both the level of the group and of the individual. Those who greedily hold to power mobilize sectarian divisions in order to reduce the complexity of natural groups; while offering the ego the delusion of its sovereignty. Certainly we see these moves in the forces of xenophobic politics which are gaining ascendency all over the globe – a symptom of a deficient and highly traumatized global consciousness; and a symptom of the rapidity of structural changes that leave us standing in interstitial space, adhering to groups promise to solidify us, at the cost of our singular and collective multiplicity. But it is also true of the progressive political forces that strip us down to unitary identity categories. If I am interpellated and pushed to identify or only recognized as gay or Latino or a psychoanalyst, I am robbed of my singularity.[21] Not as an individual, who stands alone, but as a multi-faceted intersubject with membership in a plurality of groups. The co-existence of these pluralities *are* the creative disruptions of totality within the self and within the collective. And in the same measure, this multiplicity becomes the bridging that can make differences tolerable and vibrant in new and unimagined re-groupings.

This kind of thinking and this kind of work is political in the root sense: it is the reconstruction of *polis*, the community of being singular plural. Hannah Arendt tied the plurality of thought to the very core of what it means to be human.[22] For her, the *polis* is more than simply the city; it is the forum of exchange for ideas, the place we represent ourselves to others and thereby to ourselves, where we come to understand who we are precisely through a vibrant exposition of our differences. But the vibrant exposition of differences – as is painfully evident to any thinking adult in this age of ascendent fascisms – can be a tricky matter at best, at worst a savage and intractable conflagration.

As psychoanalysts – whose method compels action in the *hic et nunc* of the transference situation – this means taking the institute itself as a site of clinical action. It is not sufficient to analyze at a distance, for we too, as a discipline are subjects of our history. And in institutional psychoanalysis this has too often been a history which has actively disavowed the domain of the social unconscious, of group relations, and the collective aspects of individual subjectivity. The institution can no longer afford to be a gated community of the mind which isolates itself from the world and so-called external reality.[23] It is the reality principle which now demands a fundamental revision of theory which incorporates the findings of group analysis and the register of the social unconscious.

Notes

[1] F. J. González, 'Trump Cards and Klein Bottles: On the Collective of the Individual', in: *Psychoanalytic Dialogues* 30 (2020), pp. 383-398. See also: F. J. González, 'Loosening the Bonds: Psychoanalysis, Feminism, and the Problem of the Group', in: *Studies in Gender and Sexuality* 13 (2012), pp. 253-267.

[2] F. Dalal, 'The Social Unconscious and Ideology: in Clinical Theory and Practice', in: *The Social Unconscious in Persons, Groups, and Societies: Mainly Theory*, Vol. I, E. Hopper, H. Weinberg (Eds.). New York: Routledge, pp. 243-264. It bears saying that the first president of the American Psychoanalytic Association, Trigant Burrow, was literally expelled because of his collectivist views. See *From Psychoanalysis to Group Analysis: The Pioneering Work of Trigant Burrow*, E. G. Pertegato & G. O. Pertegato (Eds.). London: Karnac, 2013, pp. lxxiv-lxxvi.

[3] D. Moss, 'On Hating in the First Person Plural: Thinking Psychoanalytically about Racism, Homophobia, and Misogyny', in: *Journal of the American Psychoanalytic Association* 49 (2001), pp. 1315-1334.

[4] For a more detailed examination, see E. Hopper, *The Social Unconscious: Speaking the Unspeakable*. New York: Jessica Kingsley Publishers, 2003.

[5] R. Kaës, *Linking, Alliances, and Shared Space: Groups and the Psychoanalyst*, A. Weller (Transl.). London: International Psychoanalytic Association, 2007.

[6] V. Volkan, 'Large-Group-Psychology in Its Own Right: Large-Group Identity and Peace-Making', in: *International Journal of Applied Psychoanalytic Studies* 10, 2013, pp. 210-246.

[7] F. Dalal, *Taking the Group Seriously: Towards a Post-Foulkesian Group Analytic Theory*. Philadelphia: Jessica Kingsley Publishers, 1998, p. 194.

[8] R. Kaës, *Linking, Alliances, and Shared Space*, p. 241.

[9] J.-L. Nancy, *The Inoperative Community*, P. Connor (Ed.); P. Connor, L. Garbus, M. Holland, S. Sawhney (Transl.). Minneapolis and Oxford: University of Minnesota Press, 1991, p. 27.

[10] T.H. Ogden, 'Ontological Psychoanalysis or "What Do You Want to Be When You Grow Up?"', in: *Psychoanalytic Quarterly* 88 (2019), pp. 661-684.

[11] K. Crenshaw, 'Demarginalizing the Intersection of Race and Sex: A Black Feminist Critique of Antidiscrimination Doctrine, Feminist Theory and Antiracist Politics',

in: *University of Chicago Legal Forum* 8, 1989, pp. 139-167. It should be said that Crenshaw's theory is a theory of layered *oppressions* (specifically being Black and a woman in the eyes of the law). The "intersectionality" of those not oppressed might better be captured by the term multiplicity.

[12] P. M. Bromberg, 'Standing in the Spaces: The Multiplicity Of Self And The Psycho-analytic Relationship', in: *Contemporary Psychoanalysis* 32 (1996), pp. 509-535.

[13] E. Pichon-Rivière, *El proceso grupal: Del psicoanálisis a la psicología social (I)*. Buenos Aires: Nueva Vision, 2003 [1985].

[14] Ibid., p. 42.

[15] S. Freud, *Civilization and its Discontents* (1930), *SE* 21, p. 57-146, p. 95.

[16] Z. Bauman, *Modernity and Ambivalence*, Cambridge, UK: Polity Press, 1991, p. 174.

[17] Ibid., p. 179.

[18] S. Freud, *Beyond the Pleasure Principle* (1921), *SE* 18, p. 1-64, p. 12

[19] In in her book, *The Clinic and the Context: Historical Essays*, New York: Routledge, 2013, Elizabeth Young-Bruehl makes the point that a global consciousness was first developed in the crucible of the world wars, but that this was then necessarily a *traumatic* global consciousness.

[20] A. Sen, *Identity and Violence: The Illusion of Destiny*. New York: Penguin Books, 2006, p. xiv (emphasis in original).

[21] "Interpellation" is, of course, Althusser's term for the kind of "hailing" of ideology apparatuses that call the subject into existence. "Individuals are always already subjects" of this ideology. See L. Althusser, 'Ideology, and Ideological State Apparatuses (Notes towards an Investigation)', *Lenin and Philosophy and Other Essays*. Verso: 1970, p. 11.

[22] H. Arendt, *The Human Condition* Chicago: University of Chicago Press, 1998 [1958].

[23] For further elaboration of these ideas, see my paper: F. J. González, 'First World Problems and Gated Communities of the Mind: An Ethics of Place in Psychoanalysis,' *The Psychoanalytic Quarterly* 89 (2020), pp. 741-770. DOI: 10.1080/00332828.2020.1805271

Mass Death / Tobacco and Salt

Ranjana Khanna

"In *Le Père Goriot*, Balzac alludes to a passage in the works of
J.-J. Rousseau where that author asks the reader what he would do if –
without leaving Paris and of course without being discovered – he could
kill, with great profit to himself, an old mandarin in Peking by a mere
act of will. Rousseau implies that he would not give much for the life
of that dignitary. 'Tuer son mandarin' has become a proverbial phrase
for this secret readiness, present even in modern man."
—Sigmund Freud, 'Thoughts for the Times on War and Death'[1]

In 1981, at the invitation of the psychoanalyst René Major, Jacques
Derrida addressed the French Latin-American meeting of the International
Psychoanalytic Association (IPA). His lecture, (which would subsequently
become the article "Geopsychoanalysis") makes a demand on the institutions
of psychoanalysis to consider its prejudices and pieties, as well as the potential
radical nature of its own legacy (and indeed the problematic category of legacy
itself). His lecture was written and delivered at the time of the dictatorship
in Argentina. What I mean by the problem of *legacy itself* (the familial,
usually the patrilineal, the proper name, private property and inheritance,
causality and the consequential, the Viennese becoming international), is
explored of course in many of Derrida's texts, perhaps most compellingly
for psychoanalysis in *The Postcard*, and the series of love-letters examining
the queer position or orientation of Socrates and Plato (Who comes first?
Whose legs are whose? Who dictates to whom? Writing before speech, or
the inverse?), the recto/verso of the postcard, the cut in the thread of legacy
understood as a product of the sexual reduced to the reproductive, and
centrally in the essay titled, "Freud's Legacy."[2] Referencing the condition of
possibility of the psychoanalytic international (as well as colonialism) as the
postal system, "Geopsychoanalysis" challenges the IPA to come to grips with
what it means to be "international" at that chapter of dictatorship, to ask what

constitutes the linguistic, political, and physical geography – and perhaps the geology – of contemporary psychoanalysis. Suggesting that the IPA's anodyne condemnation of torture in Latin America is a betrayal of the letter, or the text, of psychoanalysis itself, Derrida writes of the IPA's incapacity to embrace *difference*, as implied by worldwide involvement in the association:

> It contemplates the 'transfer' (the exact word used) of the IPA's property, i.e., the passing down of the only possible, perceptible, preservable legacy of the organisation. To whom, then, is this legacy to be transferred? [...] [T]he IPA cannot be dissolved by correspondence or by telegram even if a majority in favor exists, nor can it be dissolved by letter, postcard, telephone, satellite relay, or telepathy, Freud's self-acknowledged conversion of 1926–1930 to *Gedankenübertragung* or thought-transfer notwithstanding. This axiomatics of presence is extraordinarily revealing here. And this, not only for what it tells us of the ontological underpinnings of the IPA Constitution but also because it is a safe bet that those today who have the most to say, and do, in connection with the transformation of the psychoanalytic international will not be able to be present.[3]

Derrida then links the problem of legacy in the institution of psychoanalysis to its blindness to the letter/s of psychoanalysis, its technologies of utterance and invitation, its reliance on the dative (an indirect object or recipient of speech), and perhaps apostrophe (an exclamation addressed to a person usually absent), and by implication, to one of its major contributions – the potential dissolution of a certain ontological framework in its understanding of the psyche. He furthermore stresses that the institutional blind-spot surrounding legacy is linked to a metaphysics of presence that makes the institution continuous with, rather than divergent from, a politics that interrogates psychoanalytically neither violence nor politico-legal fervour at the level of the local or regional (Latin-American) nor the global (international, or "the rest of the world").

Derrida's address concerns Latin America as both a site of contemporary torture, and of a flourishing psychoanalytic culture. Given the political climate of the region, he also addresses the name "Latin America" as a signifier of torture. Derrida's demand on the IPA is to consider what torture means for psychoanalysis beyond that articulated in the liberal and general terms of its statement on the topic in response to torture in Latin America.

He tackles head-on the issue of institutional statements more broadly, and thus provides a salutary commentary on our current historical moment, which is characterised by the declarative statement in which many around the world have issued condemnations of police violence in support of the Black Lives Matter movement, or of the situation in the Palestinian occupied territories of the West Bank or Gaza Strip, for example. Statements frequently rehearse liberal sentiment on the subject of human suffering that are perhaps "better than nothing" but do little to make the statement accountable to what is most challenging and generative in psychoanalysis – namely the potential to criticise the pieties of liberal paradigms of politics.[4] Do more and indeed say more in the face of "the unutterable horror of violence, torture, and extermination", Derrida suggests.[5] The anodyne platitudes may be "better than nothing" but do nothing to bring psychoanalytic thinking to bear on the categories of liberal human rights operations, nor to challenge psychoanalysis to reform itself and dignify the letter of psychoanalysis. Nor do those platitudes sufficiently challenge psychoanalysis as a potential conduit of violence. Refuse such appropriation by forces of violence, he seems to be demanding, and acknowledge that human rights operations themselves carry their own logic of violence. Psychoanalysis, he contends, must question the dissociation between the sphere of life generally addressed by psychoanalysts – on the one hand, the intimate, the personal, the drives and the desires; and on the other hand the notion of a citizen or a subject who acts in the world and is thus part of a group, mass, or local and world population. In addition, he invites the institution of psychoanalysis to better interrogate the idea of human rights and the notions of personhood, humanity and dignity and the rights-bearing citizen addressing what justice and other philosophemes mean, in the context of psychoanalysis. While the statement by the IPA suggests that psychoanalysis has a rigorous discourse on nonviolence, Derrida insists that the psychoanalytic ethico-political position is less clear on the issue. Psychoanalysts need to own up to the radical implications for politics comprised in the text of psychoanalysis, he suggests, and participate in the deconstruction of political philosophy. He writes:

> [S]helter is taken behind a language with no psychoanalytical nature and that should certainly satisfy no one present here today. What is an 'individual'? What is a 'legitimate freedom' from a psychoanalytical point of view? How is *habeas corpus* defined? What does it mean to exclude all political aims? What is a political aim? And so on. Even if it is not to be condemned – because it is better than nothing – falling back upon the

appeal to human rights seems an inadequate response in at least three ways. I pass quickly over the first, the most radical, which is bound up with the philosophy of law, its history, the problem of its relationships to ethics, politics, ontology, and the value of the person or even of the humanity of the human individual – the possibility (or impossibility) of forming the notion of a dignity (*Würdigkeit*), in the Kantian sense, which would transcend all values, all exchange, all equivalence, all *Marktpreis*, and perhaps even go beyond the idea of law itself, beyond judicial weighing-up: so many vast and pressing issues which the psychoanalytical problematic should no longer be able to evade and about which it ought to open a debate with Plato, Kant, Hegel, Marx, Heidegger, and several others, as well as with jurists and philosophers of law. A debate of this kind has never been more *apropos*, and when I say that psychoanalysis should no longer be able to evade it, this also implies, in my view, that psychoanalysis cannot itself in this respect be evaded.[6]

Pressing the question of what psychoanalysis demands, Derrida further stresses an engagement with its potential in the analysis of mass violence and thus on a commentary on human rights:

> What in psychoanalysis is non-analogous, what is it that's unique to psychoanalysis, that cannot be assimilated into the rubric of some other form of care? First and foremost, it is a deep questioning of the category of both human and right, and indeed the geographical mapping of the world that (after Heidegger) "wipes out the Earth" as site of inscription. If no ethical discourse has incorporated the axiomatics of psycho-analysis, no political discourse has done so either.[7]

To try to understand Derrida's claim that psychoanalysis's exceptionality is its "deep questioning of the category of both human and right, and indeed the geographical mapping of the world", I now want to turn to Freud's 'Thoughts for the Times on War and Death'.

The two essays written in March and April 1915, and published as 'Thoughts for the Times on War and Death', provide for an understanding of group affiliation. These occur on the scale of the national or even the global, for example in what he describes as the fraternity formed among "civilised countries".[8] These thoughts on the masses emerge in the context of war and of increased disappointment and disillusionment on behalf of a *we*, or of a generalised

Man (translated as "one") that also challenges the possibility of the continued existence of that *we* imagined as a people represented by a government. Indeed, what constitutes a tolerable life in the face of the intolerable exigencies of that which is performed in the name of civilisation reveals what is at stake in living, whether in affiliation to a group or in the rejection of that group. Freud ends 'Thoughts for the Times on War and Death' with a commentary on the intolerable nature of the war that has resulted in tens of thousands dying daily, concluding that:

> To tolerate life remains, after all, the first duty of all living beings. Illusion becomes valueless if it makes this harder for us. We recall the old saying: *Si vis pacem, para bellum*. If you want to preserve peace, arm for war. It would be in keeping with the times to alter it: *Si vis vitam, para mortem*. If you want to endure life, prepare yourself for death.[9]

'Thoughts for the Times on War and Death' was Freud's attempt to make sense of widespread disillusionment concerning civilisation, the laws of war, and ideals of peace. This disillusionment is signalled through his use of the first-person plural, as well as his generalisations about "countless men and women" juxtaposed with "the individual". In this juxtaposition, he considered how to orient oneself (sometimes quite explicitly in spatial terms as vertigo or as a loss of footing) in relation to mass death. He writes, "The individual who is not himself a combatant – and so a cog in the gigantic machine of war – feels bewildered in his orientation, and inhibited in his powers and activities."[10] In the first essay, without directly citing, he stages readings of Thomas Hobbes's state of nature from the *Leviathan* and Immanuel Kant's *Of Perpetual Peace*, classic texts on statehood and the social contract that constitute the philosophical basis of international law. Freud then writes of his own disillusionment with the turn to war as a solution to political strife, and of the paradoxical inevitability of war in the face of a legal apparatus for perpetual peace, among what he understood to be advanced societies. Freud attributes this loss of an ideal to the betrayal of an understanding of civilisation, such as the one presented in museums in which one observes a carefully documented and enshrined heritage. This forms the basis of an ideology of a division of lands. In civilisation, one understands oneself as belonging to the world of peace with all the hospitality afforded by that term. In actuality, war is perpetual. The laws of peace are the laws of war. In this context of the idea of a civilised group of nations he writes:

> [...] countless men and women have exchanged their native home for a foreign one, and made their existence dependent on the intercommunications between friendly nations. Moreover, anyone who was not by stress of circumstance confined to one spot could create for himself out of all the advantages and attractions of these civilised countries a new and wider fatherland, in which he could move about without hindrance or suspicion.[11]

The international laws of war and peace thus allow for a sense of belonging and movement (hospitality) across borders, at least for some members of civilisation. For Freud – himself a true internationalist of sorts – this arrangement begs the question of the forms of unhappiness in civilisation produced to ensure the rights of private property and the advance of capital, and to differentiate between those with common bonds based on established legal and institutional values, and the lives demarcated by those very values that exist outside their parameters. He writes:

> Peoples are more or less represented by the states which they form, and these states by the governments which rule them. The individual citizen can with horror convince himself in this war of what would occasionally cross his mind in peace-time – that the state has forbidden to the individual the practice of wrongdoing, not because it desires to abolish it, but because it desires to monopolise it, like salt and tobacco. A belligerent state permits itself every such misdeed, every such act of violence, as would disgrace the individual. It makes use against the enemy not only of the accepted *ruses de guerre*, but of deliberate lying and deception as well – and to a degree which seems to exceed the usage of former wars. The state exacts the utmost degree of obedience and sacrifice from its citizens.[12]

'Thoughts for the Times' provides a specifically temporal dimension to the idea of the group – something presented in the use of the first-person plural "we", which, in the context of mass disaster or mass death in times of war is shaped through a series of oppositions that emerge troubled in Freud's writing. 'Thoughts for the times' (*Zeitgemäßes*) announces this temporal dimension etymologically, bringing together time and the group through the time of the mass (or congregation), or how that which emerges as a "we" is heralded in a particular moment through thought and speculation that may bring about that group's potential dissolution. The group, in that context, is one that exists within the confines of amity, and secondly in a rapport of political affiliation with the nation.

The translator of the English edition James Strachey uses the first person plural numerous times in the essay: when Freud uses the neutral pronoun *man*, Strachey often shifts between *one* and *we*; and the generalised *man* is appropriately rendered as shifting between a collective "one" effectively as the collective form of "I", or people like me and that false pronoun, *we*. Thus *man* or *we* is indicated both as what had been (through the pluperfect "hatte man erwartet") and what (in the second essay) might be again, that is, what stands in speculation in the face of death. The German pronoun *man* exists only in the nominative form, namely, as the subject of a sentence:

> We had expected the great world-dominating nations of white race upon whom the leadership of the human species has fallen, who were known to have world-wide interests as their concern, to whose creative powers were due not only our technical advances towards the control of nature but the artistic and scientific standards of civilisation – we had expected these peoples to succeed in discovering another way of settling misunderstandings and conflicts of interest.[13]

The *we* here are those who have entered a contract with the sovereign, such that in exchange for protection, *we* must be willing to die for the nation.

As the linguist Benveniste has argued, the *we* or nominally first-person plural is a false plural, precisely because the *I* announces a singularity in time – in an "instance of discourse" – that cannot in any simple way be pluralised (even in the context of an idea of fluidity of being, for example).[14] In the debates around ontogeny and philogeny in Freudian thought is then a sociogeny (as Frantz Fanon would put it) always present from which the *I* emerges – there can be no *I* without context. But this sociogeny of mass death also gives rise to a speculative form that emerges as a way of reaching the possibility of an individuated tolerable life next to the corpse, and in a moment of speculation concerning the group itself.

> Philosophers have declared that the intellectual enigma presented to primeval man by the picture of death forced him to reflection, and thus became the starting-point of all speculation. I believe that here the philosophers are thinking too philosophically, and giving too little consideration to the motives that were primarily operative. I should

like therefore to limit and correct their assertion. In my view, primeval man must have triumphed beside the body of his slain enemy, without being led to rack his brains about the enigma of life and death. What released the spirit of enquiry in man was not the intellectual enigma, and not every death, but the conflict of feeling at the death of loved yet alien and hated persons.[15]

In other words, the moment of being beside the corpse, or a mass of corpses, brings a form of speculation concerning affiliations in the group that had been suspended by the law and by the sovereign. In this understanding of spatial proximity, Freud continues and then generates further a legacy of how philosophers make use of visual technologies of imaging the corpse. Images of corpses, with living people in proximity to them, become important in the understanding of aesthetic mediation and speculation in Freud more broadly, looking back to the work of Hegel, and forward to that of Derrida, Irigaray, Spivak, and Kofman in the context of surviving the intolerable.[16]

Published in 1915, 'Thoughts for the Times on War and Death' is a relatively early contemplation of the group (a *we* or an *us* in opposition to a *them*) in Freud's work, and links its conceptualisation to loss and deprivation. It certainly builds explicitly on the anthropological ethos of *Totem and Taboo* (1912–13), and yet it is different in tone, referencing the primitive without being primarily anthropological, and attempting a form of thinking ontogeny, philogeny, and sociogeny through the rubric of the disappointment that comes with disillusionment. It foreshadows the idea in 'Mourning and Melancholia' (1916/17 [1915]) that the loss of an ideal (not necessarily a person, but a cherished ideal such as peace) might come with an impoverishment of ego, and in doing so muddies the waters between "loss of an ideal" on the one hand (which seems to be conceived in terms of the secular) and disillusionment (or the loss of an illusion) that is later perceived in relation to religion, or to the rejection of it.

Disappointment, or the loss of an ideal, manifests itself in terms of scale in times of war, in which nothing seems like it was. He writes in reference to the expectation of peace established in International Law and European amity lines, implicitly of such political conditions as the Pax Britannica – the period of general world peace in the nineteenth century when the British became the world's police – criminalising activity by claiming a monopoly on it, and thereby establishing themselves as sovereign, and thus outside the law. When we acknowledge how this Pax Britannica was built upon European amity lines in the early period of international law, we must also think back to the implicit justification for colonial expansion conveyed in Kant's *Of Perpetual Peace*, or jump forward to Carl Schmitt's fears of the American *nomos* over the planet in the post-World War II period.[17]

While not explicitly a theorisation of the group, 'Thoughts for the Times' implies the synthetic shift in individual and group through the two sections of the essay, the first of which addresses war, or the loss of ideals in relation to large groups – "the civilised people of the world", as distinct from primitive peoples; the second section speculates on the transformative experience of the death of a loved one, and the sense of bellicose affiliations that shape that (individuated) experiences of friend and enemy (and thus, indeed, the proximity between the civilised and the primitive.) Whether (and how) we can experience mass death is of course very much a question of our times, which are characterised also by sirens and body-bags from pandemics, police and state violence, war, and the proliferation of images of corpses, or of bodies becoming corpse, divested of their humanness. The essay asks us to contemplate whether "the mass" can be figured only through the manner in which an individual carries the trace of their affiliation to a group, such that the first-person plural becomes a possibility.

'Thoughts for the Times on War and Death' elaborates on how the experience of mass death shifts one's understanding of individual death, and vice versa. Conceived as a primitive relation between loved ones and enemy combatants (of group identifications and cathexes), the fundamental distinction between life and death occurs through the experience of being next to the corpse (indeed, the moment of speculation is one in which one is oriented beside the corpse). Disillusionment in the face of body-bags disturbs the relations among a band of brothers, exposing the order that they established as one based on a violent fantasy of the sexual greed of the father, rather than a crime of deprivation of pleasure. Elaborating on the friend – enemy distinction through *Totem and Taboo*, Freud provides implicit notions of the political as they unfurl in relation to mourning and the group, the perversity of amity lines and national borders in relation to global problems (such as a rampant virus or a climate crisis) through group identification, and the question of individual agency in relation to mass death.

The essay blurs the distinction between error and belief in the context of a relationship to the sovereign. In 1927, in *The Future of an Illusion*,[18] Freud distinguishes between these two different registers thus – scientific beliefs such as "Aristotle's belief that vermin are developed out of dung"[19] are errors. But, he writes, "the assertion made by certain nationalists that the Indo-Germanic race is the only one capable of civilisation" is an illusion. "Illusions need not necessarily be false", he writes, but "what is characteristic of illusions is that they are derived from human wishes."[20] The 1915 essay, however, begs a consideration of what form of speculation arises from being beside a corpse, in the context of the mass death of World War I, or indeed in peacetime during slavery (tobacco, for example in the southern United States, the Caribbean, and Brazil), or colonialism (salt, for example in the context of the British monopoly in India).

He writes the essay to express his own disillusionment in a political system that had insisted that it was in place to protect its people, and that within the "civilised nations of the world" the laws of peace would protect against mass death. He writes that with the onset of war with tens of thousands of citizens of civilised states dying each week, comes the realisation that states wanted the monopoly on the bellicose state of nature that resides in everyone, thus criminalising acts and practices at the individual level in order to claim those acts as the right of the state. With the shift from trade to policies of mercantilism (and colonialism to imperialism), they did not want simply to protect and did not have the means, even less the desire, to negotiate peace. Freud describes primitive man who knew his enemy as Other and had no problem killing him, even as he imagined himself to be beyond death. The crisis for Freud's primitive, however, comes at the moment in which a loved one is killed.

Freud refers to Aristotle, who, in *De Anima* suggests that a dead body, or a corpse, appears more like a statue of a body than it is like a real body. It looks like a body, perhaps, but it is not, in fact, a body at all. Aristotle writes: "The body which has lost its soul is not the one which is potentially alive; this is rather the one which has a soul."[21] Aristotle suggests that on looking at the corpse, we provide comfort for ourselves. Claiming that this contemplation of the corpse is the beginning of speculation, Aristotle thus provides what Freud would call an illusion: a religious rationalisation that helps us believe, as we contemplate a corpse, that it is not our loved one. He or she has gone elsewhere (as a soul, or anima). And we are left, thus, with a shell, or a sculpture.

Freud explains how it is that modern war has changed our attitude toward death, such that these illusions are palpably figurative attempts to make sense of that which is incomprehensible to the self – its ultimate other – i.e., death. He says that while modern man may when next to the corpse, be comforted that the loved one is not in this rotting carcass, primeval man is in a different relation of disavowal when he stands next to the corpse of a loved one and must read it as Other (like the enemy he kills with ease), and like himself (who cannot believe in his own death).

It might be said that we owe the fairest flowerings of our love to the reaction against the hostile impulse which we sense within us. To sum up: our unconscious is just as inaccessible to the idea of our own death, just as murderously inclined towards strangers, just as divided (that is, ambivalent) towards those we love, as was primeval man. But how far we have moved from this primal state in our conventional and cultural attitude towards death! It is easy to see how war impinges on this dichotomy. It strips us of the later accretions of civilisation, and lays bare the primal man in each of us. It compels us once more to be heroes who cannot believe in their own death.[22]

The standing alongside the dead other, then gives rise to a form of speculation, perhaps a form of reading, that allows us to understand both a dimension of height or deference (understood as respect for and reverence toward the sanctified dead) and a dimension of disavowal as we name and deface the Other who is not the enemy as such. As for the primitive, there is no unconscious experience of one's own death. Contemplation next to the corpse does not lie within the limits of recognition, but rather in the attempt to understand the other as the corpse, we are expected to acknowledge both our love (it is like us, and therefore cannot die), and our murderous impulse toward it,

> [...] for every injury to our almighty and autocratic ego is at bottom a crime of *lèse-majesté* [crime against a sovereign power]. And so, if we are to be judged by our unconscious wishful impulses, we ourselves are, like primeval man, a gang of murderers. It is fortunate that all these wishes do not possess the potency that was attributed to them in primeval times; in the cross-fire of mutual curses mankind would long since have perished, the best and wisest of men and the loveliest and fairest of women with the rest.[23]

In the moment of speculation next to the corpse, *we* present ourselves, then, to ourselves as disillusioned as a way of dispelling the fact that war is a time of having to conceal the lust to kill even our loved ones by insisting again on the laws of peace that have nonetheless permitted war. Disillusionment is thus a form of concealment of the desire to kill within the group. The crime of that impulse must be concealed through the law, and the law allows for a shift from filiation (or negotiating the fraternal and the law in the anthropological *Totem and Taboo*) to congregation (in relation to an illusion of religion and afterlife, and the idea, cited earlier, that war happens only because of different levels of equality – something that Freud takes from Trotter, but then departs from) and then to affiliation (or the group, in which a relation of introjection, projected as cannibalism, permits the subject, paradoxically, to achieve sovereignty).

In Freud's final work, *Moses and Monotheism,* we come to understand how the law (and thus crime) are established with man seeking out the fraternal bond (and not, as we might gather from *Totem and Taboo,* that the crime of killing the father initiates the production of law to guarantee peace among the brothers.). *Moses and Monotheism* gives us insight into how an inversion is at the origin of religion (the denial of the murder of the foreigner Egyptian Moses), religion provides a balm in the shape of commandments, national affiliation or affiliation to civilisation, the laws of peace and war, and thus ones from kinship to society, and the idea of an ego ideal that has to be constituted, through slaying, in order to avoid mass death. However, read alongside 'Thoughts for the Times', we can see that in fact they establish the basis for mass death that becomes apparent in the arrival of body-bags. In his reading of Freud's *Totem and Taboo,* Lacan put it thus: "If it is true that there can only be an act in a context already replete with everything involving the signifier's effect, its entry into the world, there can be no act in the beginning at least none that could be described as murder."[24] The murder is thus both effect and cause of the law – in other words, a sovereign act – a birth of the 'I'. Hence, Lacan concludes that "This myth can have no other sense here than the one I have reduced it to, a statement of the impossible".[25] It is, then, a prosopopoeia – which is always about the presence and absence of the emerging yet unrealisable face.

Orientation next to the corpse, then, provides the occasion to speculate into the intolerable at the heart of the group – both the death of the self, conceived individually and as part of a collective, and the living of the Other.

Returning briefly to Derrida through his essay "Psychoanalysis Searches the State of its Soul" (2000), we see once again an appeal to psychoanalysts for a psychoanalysis without alibi in the context of its "worldwide-isation". As in "Geopsychoanalysis", Derrida addresses the international group of analysts at the invitation of René Major. Naming the IPA the "States General of Psychoanalysis", Derrida points to a monarchical structure in the idea of psychoanalysis. Alluding to the French Revolution, through *paregicide,* the States General will dissolve at the moment of revolution – the transformation of the States General would turn into a National Constituent Assembly. Derrida asks, "More than two centuries later [after the French revolution] is the meeting of a States General of Psychoanalysis destined to save or condemn a king or a father of the nation? Which king, which father, which nation?"[26]

Calling on the States General to understand the different manifestations of sovereign cruelty and capitalist monopoly (on tobacco, salt, the state of nature, for example), we have an encounter with the colonial other, as if the Haitian Revolution was hanging in the sidelines of that dominant story of the rights of man. Worldwide-isation would require psychoanalysis to search the state of its soul and the way in which it has not only sidelined the rest of the world, but as with its colonial powers at the moment of revolution, how this process left a monarchical structure in place in its attitude towards it. The extractivism of colonialism and slavery in the context of tobacco and salt, and the act of making life disposable in the context of war, is indeed part of the history of liberal inclusion and expansion. But the fundamental crisis of "the rest of the world" is the disappointment in recognition of a contradiction in that idea of "man" when it comes to the colonies. If Derrida is thinking of his own ancestry in Algeria when he refers to Fanon in "Geopsychoanalysis", and to the ironies of the French Revolution in the context of emerging colonial interests in Algeria, Karima Lazali's book on *Colonial Trauma* similarly bears out this problem of understanding the world and its humans as a group, and indeed the exigencies of the friend–enemy equation. If the shared secret of the tyrannical father pre-empts fratricide, the guilt of parricide forbids the enjoyment of that which the father forbade. As Lazali puts it, "the trace of a memory [...] curbs the son's murderous desires such that the community of brothers is founded on the taboo of murder and incest."[27] Sometimes, Lazali reminds us through Freud's reference to Atkinson, the opposite happens, and the killing does not stop – patricide begets fratricide when there is no trace of memory. Lazali is thinking of the continuation of the monarchical structure in the colonies following the French revolution – the king's two bodies continue, but out of the hexagon and into Algeria, and this monarchical principle at the heart of the colonial presence in Algeria has an effect in the form of various traumatic repetitions through the erased memory of this founding sovereign gesture. Effectively, the two bodies of sovereign cruelty take the place of the disappeared memories and corpses of mass death in Algeria, and in Argentina, leaving one in the impossible situation of no orientation toward the corpse, and the empty crypt of un/translatability.

Death and loss, then, are configured in the founding texts of psychoanalysis, in terms of the group, indeed the mass, and the relation to the figure who is imagined to be the origin of the group whose death orients the group members relationships to each other. Laws are established in relation to that misrecognised ego-ideal, whose cruelty becomes the foundation of the laws that bind the group together in self-recognition and in opposition to those that are not part of it, nor privy to its laws or to civilisation, nor to the idea of peace, which they have experienced only as monopoly over goods and the cruelty of being. The "rest of the world" is subjected then to the production of death in the laws of war in which an imagined enemy combatant provides an alibi for the right of the sovereign to grant belonging or expulsion from the group.

Notes

[1] S. Freud, 'Thoughts for the Times on War and Death (1915)', *SE* 14, pp. 273-300, p. 298.

[2] J. Derrida, *The Post Card: From Socrates to Freud and Beyond*, A. Bass (Transl.). Chicago: University of Chicago Press, 1987.

[3] J. Derrida, 'Geopsychoanalysis: "... And the Rest of the World"', D. Nicholson-Smith (Transl.), in: *American Imago* 48/2 (1991), pp. 199-231.

[4] Ibid., p. 210.

[5] Ibid., p. 201.

[6] Ibid., pp. 215-216.

[7] Ibid., p. 214.

[8] S. Freud, 'Thoughts for the Times on War and Death', p. 277.

[9] Ibid., pp. 299-300.

[10] Ibid., 275.

[11] Ibid., p. 277.

[12] Ibid., p. 279.

[13] Ibid., p. 276.

[14] É. Benveniste, 'The Nature of Pronouns' and 'Subjectivity in Language', in: *Problems in General Linguistics.* Coral Gables, FL: University of Miami Press, 1971, pp. 217-222; pp. 223-230.

[15] S. Freud, 'Thoughts for the Times on War and Death', p. 293.

[16] See G. W. F. Hegel, *The Phenomenology of Spirit*, A.V. Miller (Transl). Oxford: Oxford University Press, 1977, p. 51; J. Derrida, 'To Speculate – on Freud', in: *Postcard*, A. Bass (Transl). Chicago: University of Chicago Press, 1987; L. Irigaray, *Speculum of the Other Woman*, G. C. Gill (Transl). Ithaca: Cornell University Press, 1985; S. Kofman, 'Conjuring Death: Remarks on *The Anatomy Lesson of Doctor Nicolas Tulp*', in: *Selected Writings*, P.-A. Brault (Transl). Stanford: Stanford University Press, 2007; G. C. Spivak, 'Speculations: On Reading Marx after Derrida', in: *Post-Structuralism and the Question of History*, D. Attridge, G. Bennington & R. Young (Eds.). Cambridge: Cambridge University Press, 1987; G. C. Spivak, 'Scattered Speculations on the Question of Value', *Diacritics* 15 (1985/4); G. C. Spivak, 'Can the Subaltern Speak? Speculations on Widow-Sacrifice', *Wedge* 7/8 (Winter/ Spring 1985), pp. 120-130.

17 C. Schmitt, *Der Nomos der Erde im Völkerrecht des Jus Publicum Europaeum*. Berlin: Duncker & Humblot, 1950.
18 S. Freud, *The Future of an Illusion* (1927), *SE* 21, pp. 1-56.
19 Ibid., p. 30.
20 Ibid., p. 31.
21 Aristotle, *De Anima* ii 1 412b 25-26.
22 S. Freud, 'Thoughts for the Times on War and Death', p. 299.
23 Ibid., p. 297.
24 J. Lacan, *The Seminar. Book XVII. The Other Side of Psychoanalysis*, R. Grigg (Transl.), New York: Norton, 2008, p. 129.
25 Ibid., p. 125.
26 J. Derrida, 'Geopsychoanalysis', p. 261.
27 K. Lazali, *Colonial Trauma: A Study of the Psychic and Political Consequences of Colonial Oppression in Algeria*. Cambridge: Polity, 2021.

Art, Identity, and Group Psychology in Digital Modernity

Sama Maani

The question I would like to ask today, and which I will try to answer to a certain degree, is whether and how the theories Freud developed in *Group psychology and the Analysis of the Ego* can substantiate the analysis of present debates on art and literature, which are often rooted in identity politics. These debates mainly happen on the Internet, a medium that is able to mobilize groups like no other. This question holds a risk that Adorno emphatically points out in his *Three Studies on Hegel*, rejecting the "impudent claim" that:

> because one has the dubious good fortune to live later [...] one can sovereignly assign the dead person his place, thereby in some sense elevating oneself above him. This arrogance echoes in the loathsome question of what [...] in Hegel [...] has any meaning for the present [...] The converse question is not even raised: what *the present means in the face of Hegel.*[1]

In our context, then, we will now proceed to ask the question what the present means in the face of the Freud of *Group Psychology and the Analysis of the Ego.* "The most remarkable and also the most important result of the formation of a group," Freud writes in reference to the psychologist William McDougall in *Group Psychology*

> is the '*exaltation or intensification of emotion*' produced in every member of it [...] [We might say] men's emotions are stirred in a group to a pitch that they seldom or never attain under other conditions; and it is a pleasurable experience for those who are concerned, to surrender themselves so unreservedly to their passions and thus to become merged in the group and to lose the sense of the limits of their individuality. The manner in which individuals are thus carried away by a common impulse is explained by McDougall by means of [...] emotional contagion [...] The fact is that the perception of the signs of an affective state is calcu-

93

lated automatically to arouse the same affect in the person who perceives them. The greater the number of people in whom the same affect can be simultaneously observed, the stronger does this automatic compulsion grow. The individual loses his power of criticism, and lets himself slip into the same affect. But in so doing he increases the excitement of the other people, who had produced this result in him, and thus the *affective charge of the individuals becomes intensified by mutual interaction* [...].[2]

To see now how we, the present, to paraphrase Adorno, "stand" in the face of the Freud of *Group Psychology,* we will best skip to the present in order to consider some examples of the identity political debates on art and literature we have mentioned, which mainly happen on the Internet.

"Execution is not art!", was a protest banner against *Scaffold,* an installation by US artist Sam Durant that had been placed in the park of the prestigious Walker Center in Minneapolis – a wooden structure critically alluding to the gallows as a "key architecture in US history".[3] Though *Scaffold* can be interpreted as a general critical reference to the practice of execution by hanging in the history of the United States, the protests exclusively understood the installation as an allusion to the largest mass execution in US history, the hanging of 38 members of the Dakota tribe after the repression of the so-called Sioux Uprising of 1862, in nearby Makato – seemingly because the installation also integrated a replica of the gallows that members of the Dakota were hanged on at the time –, and resulted in Durant feeling he had to comply with the protesters' demands and "bury" his own work of art.[4]

The second exemplary case of an art debate rooted in identity politics I want to mention is the controversies surrounding the painting *Open Casket* that was presented at the Whitney Biennial in New York in 2017. At the time, the – black – British artist Hannah Black demanded that the painting by – white – painter Dana Schutz, inspired by a photo of the body of 15-year-old Emmett Till, a black boy lynched by white racists, should not only be removed from the Whitney Biennial in New York, but also be destroyed. "I am writing to ask you", writes Black addressing the curators of the Whitney Biennial, "to remove Dana Schutz's painting 'Open Casket' and with the urgent recommendation that the painting be destroyed and not entered into any market or museum". For, Black continues, "the subject matter is not Schutz's". This case, too, caused a heated debate on the Internet, in particular on Twitter.[5]

When we confront these two debates with the quoted passage from *Group Psychology* – before going on to consider a case of a debate on literature grounded in identity politics at the end of this lecture – a conspicuous part of Freud's argument is the *intensification of emotion,* which also mentions that it can be a "*pleasurable* experience" to "surrender [...] so unreservedly to [one's] passions and thus to become merged in the group", as well as the intensification of the "affective charge [...] by mutual interaction" he calls "emotional contagion".

The "groups" we are confronted with in the context of the Sam Durant or Dana Schutz debates, however, are different from those that the Freud of *Group Psychology* and his intellectual forebears like McDougall or Le Bon were thinking of. And here the question arises whether it isn't actually absurd to say about the Internet that it is a medium that is able to mobilize *masses* like no other – for the trivial reason that the Internet is either consumed by highly isolated individuals in their living rooms, or in the public space via smartphones, where Internet users clearly signal that they do not want to be disturbed by their, to speak with Freud, fellow human beings ("Nebenmenschen") – so we are tempted to use the paradox term of "atomized masses" for these masses mobilized via the Internet.

But let's put this question aside for the moment – we will return to it later – and return to Freud's text to confront it with the problem of how it actually happens that the emotions are "stirred in a group to a pitch", and thus whether Freud's *Group Psychology* provides a *closer determination* of the context between group formation and phenomena like this pleasurable unreserved surrender of the group members to their passions.

In fact, we encounter this closer determination in Chapter IV of *Group Psychology,* where Freud starts from the hypothesis that "love relationships [...] constitute the essence of the group mind", and then attempts to explain group psychology by means of the libido theory – going on, in Chapter V and finally in Chapter XII, to apply the libido theory approach to two of what Freud calls artificial or stable groups, the Church and the army.

Regarding the libidinal structure of followers of the Church, Freud mentions two libidinal positions, both given with group formation: on the one hand the *object-love* for Christ (more exactly, the love for Christ as an *ideal,* even more exactly the replacement of the Ego ideal by the object Jesus Christ), on the other hand the *identification* with other Christians (an analogous libidinal structure, according to Freud, exists in the army: identification with other soldiers on the one hand, on the other the love for the idealized commander-in-chief).

Sama Maani

Freud writes

> Every Christian loves Christ as his ideal and feels himself united with
> all other Christians by the tie of identification. But the Church requires
> more of him. He has also to *identify* himself with Christ and love all other
> Christians as Christ loved them. At both points, therefore, the Church
> requires that the position of the libido [...] should be supplemented.
> Identification has to be added where object-choice [i.e. object-love for
> Christ] has taken place, and object-love where there is identification.[6]

The (libidinal) position of the Christian subject towards Christ thus is (or
is supposed to be) double: on the one hand defined by the object-love for
Christ, on the other hand in addition by identification with him. Or, in order
to express it in the language of Freud's second theory of drives developed in
On Narcissism: an Introduction in 1914: For the ideal-typical believer Christ is
cathected with object libido as well as (through identification) with narcissistic
libido.

Now, the libidinal position of the Christian individual towards Christ
shows an – in my opinion elucidating – analogy with the libidinal structure
of the representatives of identity politics. In order to put my argument across,
I will try to sketch a – for reasons of time foreshortened, schematic and
compressed – *genealogy of identity-political thinking*. In so doing, I will base
myself on the leftist Syrian theoretician Sami Alkayial, whose theories on the
socio-economic backgrounds of the emergence of (leftist or rather "leftist")
identity-political discourses are, I think, a good basis for discussion of the
subject – even though I feel some of Alkayial's arguments are open to criticism.

Alkayial argues:

> When capitalist societies entered the post-industrial era [at the end of
> the 1970s], this was accompanied by the *declining importance of the
> working class in social production*. The closure of factories and mines in
> the industrial cities of Great Britain or the German Ruhr region was the
> end of a world to which the traditional Left belonged. In a capitalism
> of, in the words of David Harvey, 'flexible accumulation', which deals
> with smaller sites of production, and in which the service sector and
> the production of consumer goods, information, and communication
> media play a far larger role, there is no longer room for a leading or
> broadly represented class.[7]

The talk of a "declining importance of the working class" and a "capitalism of flexible accumulation," however, seems problematic to me because it is not far removed from claims like "there is no working class anymore," or, even more radical, "there is no capital relationship anymore" – and therefore I would interpret these propositions of Alkayial as a description of the *subjective view* of many leftist and progressive activists *in reaction to real socio-economic transformations*. The fact that, in the subjective view of many leftists, the importance of the working class or the concept of class itself has declined due to the mentioned objective socio-economic transformations since the late 1970s, is probably uncontested.

These developments, Alkayial suggests, have led to an existential crisis in the thought and action of the Left. Until then, the emancipation of the working class had been closely linked to the one of the *whole* society – and thus also to the emancipation of many other oppressed and marginalized groups, for instance women or African American people in the US, and to some extent also homosexuals. On the other hand, many representatives of these groups also held leftist views. A prominent example is Martin Luther King, who, a fact that is not widely known, was in Memphis on April 3, 1968 in order to call for a general strike at a mass rally in support of striking waste workers, which aimed to paralyze all of Memphis. The next day, he was shot on the balcony of his hotel.

With the "declining importance of the working class" in the minds of many leftists, according to Alkayial, the link between the concerns of these oppressed groups and the demands of the working class began to unravel in the thought and actions of progressive actors. And the more the concept of the working class lost in "discursive weight," the more substantial seemed the discourse of these marginalized groups – and over the years it increasingly came to dominate the progressive political discourse as a whole. What is more: with the surrender of the concept of the emancipation of the working class as a "key project" in the great project of emancipating society, the idea of liberating *all of* society as such began to wane. Class theoretical terms were usurped by concepts and terms in the context of these marginalized and oppressed groups – namely the "identity" of these groups. This, according to Alkayial, can be considered the birth of identity politics (note: I do not mean to propose a nostalgic idealization of the class concept, which is also open to some criticism. This, however, is not what we are dealing with here.)

*   *   *

Let us now consider the aforementioned analogy between the libidinal position of the devout Christian towards Christ and the libidinal structure of the proponents of identity politics. The ideal-typical believer, according to Freud, firstly takes the position of object-love towards Christ, and secondly s/he identifies with Christ (or should identify with him – think of the imitatio Christi, "come, follow me"). This second libidinal position of identification then corresponds to a cathexis of the object Christ with *narcissistic libido*. Simplifying somewhat, identification with Christ involves an "integration of the object Christ" into the Ego of the faithful, linked to an *increase in narcissistic libido* – at the expense of object libido. Translated into everyday language, what happens is an increase in self-respect and pride at the expense of the interest in material objects in the external world, i.e. in a "good life". For identification with Christ cannot just mean that the faithful loves his fellow believers as much as Christ loves them ("Whatever you did for one of these least brothers of mine, you did for me", says the Gospel of Matthew), it can also lead to *pride* in one's own Christ-like virtue – together with narcissistic-ascetic ideals – and thus to the ascetic renunciation of the good life and pride in this renunciation.

In its narcissistic dimension, the libidinal position of the identification with Christ shows a clear analogy with the libidinal position of the proponents of identity politics towards "their" collective. I suggest that, for proponents of identity politics, it is not, as persistent rumours would have it, about eliminating injustice and oppression and a real improvement of the social situation of "their" collective (such an interest in a real material improvement would correspond to the object-libidinal position). Rather, it is almost the opposite: the – narcissistic – profit they gain *for themselves* by *simply addressing* the oppression of these collectives. Identity politicians like the already-mentioned Hannah Black jealously guard this narcissistically cathected issue and its "exclusive ownership" like a treasure. The trivial question where proponents of identity politics (in this case Hannah Black, a British artist who lived in Berlin at the time of the controversy) derive their legitimacy from, speaking as they do for the members of "their" collective (in this case millions of African American people in the US), is, to my knowledge, hardly ever asked.

If we think it through to the end, identity politics amounts to enshrining discrimination, as African American political theorist Adolph L. Reed has superbly demonstrated. For decades now, Reed has been writing against "race reductionism"[8] and the kind of identity politics that depicts African American people as a homogenous group by blanking out the issue of class, and its beneficiaries, who were – and continue to be – black elites, as he already was able to demonstrate in 1979 for the period between the (late) 1960s and the end of the 1970s. And this while the social and economic situation of underprivileged African Americans – according to the parameters of employment, purchase power, quality of housing, and life expectancy Reed used – continued to deteriorate.[9]

Also, and particularly in their encounters with art, proponents of identity politics remain fixated on their Ego– an Ego that for its part is identified with an imaginary collective –, insofar as what is shown seems to "trigger" certain affects in connection with "their" collective in a narcissistic-offending manner. An "offence" in this sense can often simply consist in the fact that someone who I do not consider to be part of "my" collective presumes to artistically engage with "my" collective. The affects triggered by the narcissistically offending work of art, which are lived out in an almost cathartic manner, are seemingly non-libidinous, but can in truth be pleasurable. We remember: Freud speaks of a "pleasurable experience […] to surrender […] unreservedly to [one's] passions". Pleasurable, however, in the sense of a *neurotic* pleasure. "all neurotic unpleasure is of that kind—pleasure that cannot be felt as such," writes Freud in *Beyond the Pleasure Principle*.[10] Incidentally, this reminds me of Gilles Deleuze who – based on Spinoza's definition of *tristitia*, or pain or unpleasure, as a passion (*passio*)[11] – speaks of *sad passions* that drive the masses to passionately commit against their own interests and for their servitude.[12]

*   *   *

Let us now return to the initial question: to what extent we can speak of groups with regard to the groups mobilized by the Internet? This is not merely about the fact that the members of the "internet mass" are isolated from each other in space. What is characteristic of the mass in digital modernity is that its members precisely do not want to experience themselves as part of a group but as *unique*. This is what has been voiced and promoted for decades by the narcissistic *imperatives of authenticity* that are omnipresent in advertising, in the culture industry, in pop-psych self-help literature etc., saying "Be yourself", "Believe in yourself", "Achieve your best self" etc.

The result of this pursuit of uniqueness, however, is not a multitude of really unique individuals who, as artists of their Ego, as it were, re-create themselves in ever-new guises, but – considering for instance the scene of so-called You Tube influencers – narcissistic tedium. A tedious monotony, or, to abstract a term from music theory, oligotony of a few types who can be found en masse. These types are then easily trackable on the Internet via Social Media, and they are the object of these attempts of manipulation. Michael Kosinski, who developed the psychometric methods that companies like the infamous *Cambridge Analytica* use, said in an interview that "a very few Facebook likes suffice to make fairly accurate statements [...] about [your] personality. From, let's say, 240 likes, even better ones than your spouse."[13] "The more precisely you characterize the individual, the more clearly you can see what he shares with many others,"[14] Gunter Gebauer and Sven Rücker write. What they all have in common is first and foremost the narcissistic pursuit of being and representing nothing but their own "authentic Ego". "You're so special – just like anybody else"[15] is the title of a Matthew Herbert song, putting this linkage into a nutshell.

Freud, says Adorno, had come up "against the fact that the innermost core on which the psychology of the single individual rests is [...] structures of the social context", such as "primitive forms of horde."[16] And in *Group Psychology*, Freud argues: "[The] group appears to us as a revival of the primal horde". According to Freud and Adorno, then, in the unconscious of each and every individual, in the innermost recesses of his "authentic Ego," we paradoxically encounter its opposite: the group. Freud's formula of the "internal foreign territory", which not only characterizes the unconscious as something foreign and strange, but also as something external, and Lacan's concept of *extimity* seem to point to the same context. When I, in a narcissistic manner, allow nothing to stand but my own "authentic Ego", and thus refuse to align myself to historically developed, socially acceptable forms and norms of the "external foreign territory" (i.e. the external reality of society), but to my own "innermost psychological cells," then this results precisely not in an unmistakable Ego but in regression into an – archaic – "group Ego".

This "tyranny of intimacy" combined with the decline of the public sphere that Richard Sennett lamented as early as the 1970s[17] has radicalized in digital modernity, and thus we are now faced with a "narcissification" of the public and the formation of virtual segmented groups or partial publics, better known as Internet filter bubbles; with increasing privatization of the public sphere and its fragmentation into privatized partial publics that cater to the narcissistic interests, opinions and needs of their users – and for their part promote the narcissistic encapsulation of individuals.

The narcissistic principle of digital modernity is also promoted by the fact that the magical idea of the omnipotence of thoughts on online platforms and Social Media, where anyone can potentially reach millions of people in no time and in an, as it were, magical manner, has almost come true. On the

Internet, say Gebauer and Rücker, (potentially) everyone has "the power that previously only a few held: that of giving a direction to the masses," so on the Internet, potentially everyone can be a leader.

But here we might take a step further and suggest that a thought that Freud only touches upon in Chapter V of *Group Psychology* and elaborates a little in Chapter VI, namely the one of "the possibility of a leading *idea* being substituted for a leader [my emphasis],"[18] has been realized in digital modernity in an almost uncanny way. In particular in identity political debates (on the Internet), we sometimes encounter the strange phenomenon that, to put it bluntly, we are unable to identify any really existing subject as the carrier of the leading idea of a particular debate. This was the case in the debate on the question of who was authorized to translate the young African American writer Amanda Gorman's inaugural poem (this is the third identity political art debate I mentioned before, more precisely a literary or translation debate). Later it became clear that Janice Deul, the fashion journalist who had launched the debate with a Dutch-language article, neither had suggested in this article – as had repeatedly been claimed – that only black people were able to translate Gorman's poem, nor had demanded that only black people should have the right to do so.[19] However – and this is essential – this "leading idea" (that nobody had argued) had very real consequences. As though this *idea without a sponsor* had mobilized a mass which, in Freud's words from *Group Psychology*, would impress people like "an unlimited power and an insurmountable peril"[20]: Its result was that the white, non-binary Dutch translator Marieke Lucas Rijneveld resigned from her translation job, which Gorman herself had commissioned her with. And that a Catalan translator, who had been commissioned with the translation of the poem, had his contract cancelled by the same publisher – with the justification that he had "the wrong profile".

Translated from German by Brita Pohl

Notes

1   T. W. Adorno, *Hegel: Three Studies*, S. Weber Nicholsen & J. J. Shapiro (Intr.), S. Weber Nicholsen (Transl.), Cambridge, MA/London: MIT Press, 1993, p. 1 (my emphasis).
2   S. Freud, *Group Psychology and the Analysis of the Ego* (1921), *SE* 18, pp. 65-144, p. 84.
3   'Dies ist keine Exekution', in: *Frankfurter Allgemeine Zeitung*, June 21, 2017.

4   Also see Sama Maani: 'Exekution ist keine Kunst!', in: Idem: *Warum ich über den Islam nicht mehr rede*, Klagenfurt: Drava, 2022. In order to avoid any misunderstanding: what is at issue here clearly is not "the Dakota tribe member's perception of art." Lately, we frequently encounter such positions in the art debates, and similar views are defended, for instance in the US, by members of the white majority as well as those of non-white minorities.

5   https://www.artnews.com/artnews/news/the-painting-must-go-hannah-black-pens-open-letter-to-the-whitney-about-controversial-biennial-work-7992/   (accessed 21-05-2023).

6   S. Freud, *Group Psychology*, p. 134 (my emphasis).

7   https://www.rosalux.de/news/id/14388/der-krieg-in-syrien-und-die-krise-der-linken-traditionen/ (accessed 17-05-2023).

8   https://daily.jstor.org/adolph-reed-jr-the-perils-of-race-reductionism/   (accessed 17-05-2023).

9   https://libcom.org/article/black-particularity-reconsidered-adolph-l-reed-jr/   (accessed on 17-05-2023).

10 S. Freud, *Beyond the Pleasure Principle*, SE 18, p. 11.

11 B. Spinoza, *Ethics*, London: J. M. Dent & Sons, 1941, p. 93.

12 G. Deleuze, *Spinoza: Practical Philosophy*, Robert Hurley (Transl.). San Francisco: City Lights Books, 1988, p. 25.

13 G. Gebauer & S. Rücker, *Vom Sog der Massen und der neuen Macht der Einzelnen*. Munich: DVA, 2019, p. 245.

14 Ibid.

15 Quoted in: Ibid.

16 T. W. Adorno, 'Lecture Thirteen', in: Idem, *Introduction to Sociology*, Ch. Gödde (Eds.), E. Jephcott (Transl.). Stanford: Stanford University Press, 2000, p. 115.

17 R. Sennett, *The Fall of Public Man*. New York: Knopf, 1977.

18 S. Freud, *Group Psychology*, p. 95.

19 https://taz.de/Debatte-um-Gedicht-von-Amanda-Gorman/!5758644/   (accessed 17-05-2023).

20 S. Freud, *Group Psychology*, pp. 84-85.

The Truths of Psychoanalysis: Defying the Lies of Psychology that Fuel the Digital Amassing of Individuals[1]

Jan De Vos

The Sigmund Freud Museum in Vienna announced the commemoration of Freud's book *Mass Psychology and the Analysis of the Ego* (1921), referring to contemporary phenomena:

> Today we live in a world characterised by a multitude of overlapping crises: climate change and the pandemic, forced migration, terrorism, wars, and the rise of authoritarian structures go along with a massive media transformation, a digital change of the structures of public space, and an alarming decline of democratic values as well as the demise of certainties long held to be self-evident.[2]

This evocation of our present-day ordeals spurred me to look back to my own past, situated in a historic timeframe not without its own overlapping crises, but surely the era preceding the digital change of the structures of public space, namely, a time before group and mass formations moved online, before the amassing and aggregation of people became an issue of AI and algorithms. When I was a child, all this was still taking place within an analogue framework. Consider this anecdote: I must have been around ten years old, attending a village festival of the movement I was part of, a Catholic youth movement. The setting is Flanders, somewhere in the second half of the 1970s. We were marching around a square, in uniform, there were flags and drums. I was thrilled, literally, I felt it in my stomach, I felt a sense of belonging, being a part of something bigger. And knowing this, realising it right then and there, only added to the experience... Looking back, today, I'm fascinated by how I was prone to being absorbed into the crowd, fascinated – and even slightly concerned – to recall these borderline proto-fascist tendencies.

Of course, I'm looking back now as someone who has studied Sigmund Freud, and clearly the most relevant reference is his book of 1921, *Mass*

Jan De Vos

Psychology and the Analysis of the Ego. There is this pertinacious but ultimately incorrect interpretation that Freud's thesis revolves around the idea that the masses revive atavistic, pre-individual instincts. As is well known, Freud eventually attempts to ground his model of the masses in the myth of the herd of brothers slaying the Primal Father. While in his book Freud indeed puts forward the idea of regression, of how modern masses seems to revive "primitive" urges and ways of reacting, he evokes this commenting on other mass theorists such as Gustave Le Bon and William McDougall, and this not without problematising the idea of a straightforward and unmediated return of archaic impulses. Consider in this respect Freud's engagement with McDougall's central question, where does the mass get organised:

> It seems to us that the condition McDougall described as the 'organisa-
> tion' of the mass can with greater justification be described in different
> terms. The task consists in conferring upon the mass the very qualities
> that once characterised the individual and that, so far as the individual is
> concerned, formation of the mass effaced. Because the individual (outside
> the primitive mass) possessed continuity, self-awareness, traditions and
> habits, a special job to do and a special place to occupy, he kept himself
> apart from others with whom he was in contention.[3]

Notably, Freud does not adhere to a simple timeframe of humanity first passing over mass formation to then evolve into more cultural forms of socialisation, out of which eventually the notion of the individual would arise. Instead, for Freud the individual seemingly precedes the mass. At the very least, for Freud the mass has something artificial and is mediated, it is not to be thought in merely archaic terms.

In truth, my anecdote also betrays a certain artificiality: after all, the timeframe concerns the late 1970s; all those flags and drums already signal a nostalgic yearning for some glorious imagined past. As such, the set-up of that village event was far from spontaneous or unmediated. In this respect one can turn to Theodor Adorno's insightful remark on Freud's *Mass Psychology*: he writes that while Freud wanted to unravel the psychological forces transforming individuals into a mass, the demagogues of the twentieth century tried to reproduce *synthetically* the bonds that Freud was looking for (by using mass communication technologies).[4] This makes me wonder: the artificiality – even *fakeness* – of us all marching around the square, is this not already reflected in my own being somehow distantiated from the event? That is, at the very moment itself, I was very aware *that I was thrilled by the feeling of belonging to something larger.* Hence, if I was being carried away, I was so in a reflective and thus mediated way.

Today, so many years after those days in uniform, I am still puzzled. For having read and re-read Freud's *Mass Psychology*, I wonder at the lure of mass identification: there was no leader, not even an idea or ideal with which I identified at the time. I'm not even sure to what degree there were a lot of horizontal identifications with the other youths involved in this crowd participation. The image that emerges now is how I solipsistically indulged in the *idea* of being carried along by the loving arms of the group, cradled in this mass embrace. Hence, when Freud writes about "the principal phenomenon of mass psychology, namely the individual's lack of freedom within the mass,"[5] I am no longer sure. Does my anecdote suggest my feeling like a little 'sovereign' amidst the mass? Or, did my being drawn in at the time kindle a sort of exalted sovereignty, something I consciously relished in that very moment itself? Of course, one could argue, perhaps precisely in my fantasy of sovereignty, I was fully in the grip of the group experience, or better, in the grip of the artificially set up event. At the very least, from a Freudian perspective, the question still remains: was I in the grip of a mass event without the typical bond Freud sketches out, that of a shared love for a leader that ignites horizontal identifications with the other members?

How to make sense of this? Just to be clear, I'm a Freudian. Actually, I'd argue we are all Freudians, even the cognitive psychologist, the analytic philosopher – only they do not know it... But that's another story, a story of Freud being unavoidable, or to put it properly, him being a Father Figure means that anyone dealing with the question "what is the human" (and who has not to deal with this question) thus has *daddy-Freud-issues.* Hence, as a Freudian – as Freudians – the thing to avoid is to relentlessly seek the leader/horizontal bond in every social relation; rather, if we don't see them, we should ask where the leader/horizontal have bonds gone to, and where they will eventually pop up. After all, Freud himself pondered over this very question when writing: "Is the leader truly indispensable so far as the essence of the mass is concerned?"[6] By putting the leader central, the issue eventually boils down to whether the leader is indispensable. Can we form a horizontal group *without* a leader? Can we bypass the leader? Can we get rid of him entirely? Yes, this argument is leading to the inevitable question: can we finally kill the Primal Father?

Here, a reference to Jacques Lacan might help. Although I'm a Lacanian, I would not say that everyone is a Lacanian: being Lacanian is a choice (but that's yet another story I won't go into here). Suffice to say, the crux of the

Jan De Vos

matter is *which* Freud, which brand of Freud do you want to engage with. Clearly, if my personal Freud is predominantly a Lacanian one, the quandary repeats itself with Lacan; that is, *which* Lacan has led me to this juncture (again, another story). Anyway, when Freud eventually suggests that the figure of the leader cannot be exceeded, this is precisely what Lacan at a certain point defies. First, to condense Freud's position: the innovative move of his *Mass Psychology*, is that *there is no such thing as "individual psychology"*. Arguably, this idea transpires through all Freud's writings, just consider the idea of the Oedipus complex, already indicating that subjectivity is always intertwined with sociality: the subject emerges within a social triangle. Hence, subjectivity is always social. One could even claim that subjectivity is always tied to mass psychology, and this is precisely where for Freud the figure of the Leader (which he connects to the Primal Father of *Totem and Taboo*) cannot be circumvented. Acknowledging all that, Lacan nonetheless aimed to rethink how subjectivity comes into being, and hence inter-subjectivity outside the Father/Leader equation. In for example his text 'British Psychiatry and the War' of 1946, Lacan praises the wartime work of psychiatrists and psychoanalysts such as Wilfred Bion and John Rickman and their attempt to initiate so-called "leaderless groups".[7] This formed the direct inspiration for Lacan to organise his own psychoanalytic movement around the so-called 'cartels', compact work groups without a leader which should form the backbone of the psychoanalytic organization. I will return briefly to Lacan's text later.[8]

Returning to the anecdote that sees me marching behind the flags and the drums, is this not a situation where a Father/Leader is absent? Or do we have here the same situation Freud describes in *Mass Psychology* concerning hypnosis, that generally speaking, people undergoing this somehow remain aware that it is "only a game", after all?[9] Might this mean that there is always some kind of self-deception involved, even a sort of auto-hypnosis? Knowing that ultimately it is merely a game, we go along with the setup and the script of the hypnosis. In this way, me marching and chanting on the village square, luring myself into a monumental feeling of belonging, was I not enacting an immersion in a grander order because I *longed* for it? Perhaps because at that precise moment a real leader figure might have shown up amidst that desired and enacted mass phenomenon. It goes without saying that this "auto-interpellation,"[10] calling upon myself to join the group, did not happen in a vacuum: myself and the other youths gathered together were "summoned" (or summoned ourselves) through a carefully orchestrated happening. It was anything but spontaneous.

Clearly, the flag-and-drums-event was scripted and choreographed in order to trigger certain group effects, even though at the time I was largely unaware of which flag I was marching behind. The conservative Catholic youth movement I had joined was an important part of the massive growth of modern youth movements in Flanders, just before and especially after World War II.[11] Here I will fast-forward: we could argue that after the rise of the masses in the nineteenth century came the surge in youth masses, this too a force that needed to be organised and contained. Particularly after World War II, in the West the period of school attendance was repeatedly extended, and only at an increasingly later age did youngsters join the workforce. On the one hand, there were the adults who brought young people together under specific religious, social, and political banners. On the other there was a "vocation awareness" of the youngsters themselves: inspired most centrally by Romanticism and realising that young people could play their own role in society, they attempted to organise youth or took part in existing structures.[12]

The Catholic youth movement in Flanders that I was part of – which was particularly strong in rural areas – was nationalist and conservative. As I learned later, the movement had had an obscure relationship with the Nazi collaborators in World War II. Our uniform comprised somewhat tellingly a brown shirt, yellow tie, black trousers and boots. We sang songs of a glorious romantic past, of the humble but brave Flemish people standing up against oppression. Admittedly, this nostalgic imagery had a strong hold on me, even though I was largely unaware of the underlying ideology (and its history), namely, the identity and nationalist objectives formulated behind the scene by adults and a small vanguard of young adherents. Hence, the background of my solipsistic being absorbed and my being thrilled at the village Fest was two-edged: a latent script with a hidden rationale that lured me in via the manifest content of the celebrative scenario with its heroic mythology – all features that as a young boy I fell for. As such, we might argue that my getting so carried away is linked to the bonus of *enjoyment* (a thrill doubtless foreseen by the adults and by the small vanguard of youngsters leading the movement?), as discussed by Freud via McDougall:

> It is possible, according to McDougall, to say that people's affects rarely (in different circumstances) rise to the heights they may attain in a mass; in fact, it is an enjoyable experience for those concerned to abandon them-selves so unreservedly to their passions and in the process be swallowed up in the mass, losing their feeling of individual separateness. McDougall explains this feeling on the part of individuals of being carried away in

terms of what he calls the 'principle of direct induction of emotion by way of the primitive sympathetic response.'[13]

But here, clearly, my enjoyment of not having to be my narrow *me* and instead to be swallowed up in the mass – the group compensating for my lack of *being* – already signals a kind of *not being absorbed*, a fake assimilation. This wished-for or longed-for inclusion, precisely in my reflective awareness, actually flips over into something narcissistic, something all too individual. This process could be described as follows: we love to blend in, we love to let ourselves go and relinquish ourselves. However, our very imagining this abandon means we have already stepped outside ourselves and resurrect as the fascinated onlooker of our own disappearance. So perhaps the enjoyment Freud refers to resides principally in this fascination and awe for the stories of individual, separate identities merging. A token of this is fascination with subliminal messages in music or in ads, and how these things supposedly work 'subconsciously'. Or the prurient notion that we are being steered by government's nudging policies designed by behavioural experts: Behold the power of science! they tell us. Much of this I have discussed elsewhere[14] as the *scientific interpellation*, namely, how science tells us who we are and how we function (*look, this is what you are*). Upon which we marvel and react with, *oh, fascinating!*, after which we repeat science's wonderful knowledge, *did you know that according to science the human being....?* Here, instead of identifying with that what science says we are (*look, this is what you are*), we in the first place identify with the scientific perspective and thus adopt a certain distance toward the supposed immediately given. However, in my youth it was not the *scientific* interpellation that held me in their grasp, it was the heroic mythological stories of Flanders that interpellated me and drew me into a reflective and gratifying immersion, a process that again involved a certain distance towards the supposed immediately given.

Now, at this point two paths open for scrutiny. On the one hand lie the fables and mythologies of the brave Flemish people as offered to us boys, by which we might attempt to discern the Oedipal and Primal Father themes they contain; on the other we have the role of what I call the 'little leaders', those who established the scenario in the first place. For our purposes here, the latter path is more relevant. As noted earlier, those 'little leaders' at the festival had a clear agenda: they wanted us to coalesce on the base of our uniforms, the coordinated marching, the drums, the collective songs. Were these effectively "social engineers", acting in full knowledge of what was needed to induce that sense of being-absorbed-into-the-crowd? The question is whether they knew this intuitively, or drew from psychology – perhaps even from an acquaintance with psychoanalysis.

Here we touch upon a critical issue in all things related to group formation, mass movements, populism and their like, an issue that seems at first sight to open a very different path than that of the aforementioned scientific interpellation: can science – in particular psychological science – be applied to induce group and mass formations? In *Mass Psychology*, at a given point Freud briefly refers to "Prussian militarism" of World War I being "un-psychological" and not appreciating the potential of human "libido". Freud even suggests that this omission was a major reason for the defeat that followed.[15] For his part, referring to the success of fascism, Adorno argued that Goebbels might have relied upon popularised readings of Le Bon, adding that the Nazi politician was nevertheless not fully aware of "the latest findings of modern depth psychology".[16] Adorno's take is above all that the masters of propaganda of fascism *unknowingly* or *naively* relied on psychological mechanisms. But this raises the question, what would have happened if they had been truly masterminds using the state of the art theories of group formation and mass psychology? This surmise reconnects to Lacan and his aforementioned text 'British Psychiatry and the War', in which he expresses his appreciation for how Bion and Rickman used psychological theories in order to steer group formations that moreover, as noted, were supposed to bypass the figure of the leader:

> One needs to take full account of the fact that a still very young psychological science was called upon to effect what one may call the synthetic creation of an army when this science had barely brought to the light of rational thought the notion of such a body, understood as a social group with an original structure.[17]

For me, reading this text of Lacan only recently – always having lent more on Lacan's better-known condemnation of psychology as a science – came a surprise: Did he really believe psychoanalysis to be a functional science that enabled direct intervention in social reality, or even synthetically manipulating it? As such, I have to say, I've come to loathe any attempt by experts (the little leaders?) to forge groups, to bring people together using so-called expert knowledge of people, of groups, particularly when the rationale stems from the notion that "people need to feel they *belong*". As such, I dislike any attempt to steer or engender (inter)subjectivity by those purporting to really know what other people need.

This quandary struck me when I began reading historical works on youth movements: the deliberative and conscious deployment of strategies to forge identities and groups via the use of uniforms, military inspired rituals, songs, images… But if, in my youth movement days, this psycho-social engineering was above all underpinned by ideological and political motives – only superficially or naively leaning on psychology as Adorno would have it – then what I take issue with above all is the kind of psycho-social engineering done by supposedly *non-ideological motives*; when the steering of (inter)subjectivity is informed by Humanist ideals and allegedly scientific insights. This is where in schools or other settings activities, events and the like are set up under the banner of "science" – and especially of psychology – saying, *it is good for young people to bond, to get together, it allows them to develop their skills and explore them in the appropriate psycho-social way.*

Notably, in the youth movement I was part of, several years after the flags and drums event described above, the nationalist Catholic agenda was abandoned in favour of a fully psychologised discourse. The youth leaders were informed that they had to take care of the mental well-being of the youngsters, and were given some basic hands-on knowledge of the psychology involved. Subsequently, during the weekly football match youth leaders began to enthusiastically encourage boys with less athletic aptitude to engage with the ball, as they were instructed that 'positive reinforcement' boosts self-esteem and motivation in children. In this way the youth movements followed in parallel what was already happening in education and schooling, and gradually succumbed to psychologizing discourses. Elsewhere I have critiqued the effects of deploying normative and 'moralising' models of mainstream psy-sciences, so suffice it here to add an aside, namely that this psychologisation of the youth movement was likely key to my decision to study psychology at university. Furthermore, I was uneasy about applauding a clumsy ball-kick from a boy who – without that outside pressure (that everybody deserved a place on the pitch) would probably not have played at all. All this eventually pushed me to a more critical approach toward psychology in general, and my reliance on psychoanalysis to develop this critique.

At this juncture, I would like to reconnect with one of the central themes of the Sigmund Freud Museum conference, namely the "massive media transformation, a digital change of the structures of public space."[18] To begin with, "psychologisation" has become a key issue in the digital and virtual world. Notably, one of the first organisations with a dedicated website was the American Psychological Association. If the inclination for self-diagnosis prompted the idea of "Dr Google", it is hardly surprising that for so-called mental issues the "Google psychologist" soon followed suit. Moreover, as the formations of subjectivity and inter-subjectivity have shifted increasingly toward the digital sphere, both individuation and subjectivation – and also group formation and socialisation – have inevitably been subsumed by algorithms and now AI. As the Argentina-born psychoanalyst Nestor Braunstein puts it, these new digital masses are constituted on the basis of profiles that reduce subjects to metadata.[19] Is this where the virtual becomes the synonym of "fake"? Meaning, we are force-fed ideas and convictions, while being digitally nudged to act in such and such a way. Pinned to a data-profile, tagged with a limited pre-set array of characteristics, we are lumped into groups, "community" bubbles, or digital echo-chambers, as this process has been called. As recent history has shown us, from there we are marshalled to vote in this or that way, or to go out on the streets and join the mob attacking whatever is deemed relevant at the moment, like the Capitol in Washington DC, for example.

Before I am accused of getting carried away with this somewhat dim picture of today's society, it is not equally true that digital technologies offer the individual a chance to escape today's omnipresent psycho-social engineering? After all, the computer evolved from a mainframe thing to a personal thing: the individual computer, arguably allows us to bypass and contest – or even quash – mass-psychological manipulations. See in this respect how the 1984 launch of the Apple Macintosh referenced George Orwell's novel, the message being that the "personal" computer would defy massification and tyranny. In the advertisement broadcast on television during the Super Bowl at Tampa Stadium in Florida, we see a woman in red running shorts and a white tank-top bearing the Apple logo.[20] Carrying a sledgehammer, she is pursued by police-like figures, and runs down the aisle of an auditorium filled with individuals dressed like automatons watching a Big Brother figure on a vast screen, where she spins the hammer and hurls it at the screen, which smashes with a massive explosion of light and smoke that blinds the audience. The commercial ends with: "On January 24th, Apple Computer will introduce Macintosh. And you'll see why 1984 won't be like *1984*."

Digitalisation therefore bringing to life the vision of Bion, Rickman, and Lacan: social aggregation without the leader? Surely this was the promise, the internet would enable egalitarian, horizontally structured and leaderless forms of organisation. Recently, Tim Berners-Lee – one of the key pioneers of the World Wide Web – has lamented both the malicious use of digital technologies "such as ad-based revenue models that commercially reward clickbait and the viral spread of misinformation," and the negative outcomes of the original attentively created benign technologies, witnessing how they have resulted in unintended detrimental results such as the "outraged and polarised tone and quality of online discourse." Nonetheless, Berners-Lee remains hopeful: "The web is for everyone," he insists, "and collectively we hold the power to change it."[21]

However, what if the Apple ad indicates that the two aberrations of digital technology cited by Berners-Lee are merely two sides of the same coin? For, what can be argued is that the technology as such is set up from a particular conception of how individuation relates to socialisation and subjectivity to inter-subjectivity, and that this underpinning leads to both intended as unintended anomalies. That query is endorsed by Fred Turner, who whilst driving around the campuses of Google and Apple in a television documentary comments:

> They don't want to show power, they don't want to become public [...] they don't believe that there is a genuine public space that they should be serving; Google, Apple, they want to build their world [...] we want to help people brand themselves [...] to engage in complex, collaborative consumption. Great. The public, what's that? People will take care of themselves...

This anti-social individualism – standing diametrically opposite Freud's vision that there is no such thing as individual psychology – fuels the imagery of Apple's personal computer. The heroine in the red running shorts is in the end merely a caricature Ayn Rand-type hero whose radical individualism – based on a total rejection of the group and the social, cannot but result in the return of the repressed: that is, the return of the mass phenomena. In this way, today, Apple's 1984 advertisement cannot but strike us as a cynical joke: the more personal our devices become, the more we are collectively in the grip of Orwell's "telescreen". Nowadays, taking the metro, one sees almost everybody glued to their personal screen, many continuing scrolling as they get off and take the stairs, and emerge into the streets... one might wonder, how on earth could one heroine smash all those screens. Is this not your typical science-fiction horror movie: slaying the monster (i.e., killing the Father figure) merely unleashes a horde of little monsters, spewing from the belly of the dead beast. Having smashed that huge screen, what we have now is the multiplication of mini-screens, with each person trapped in their solipsistic first-person perspective, while watching some mass-culture product.

As the French philosopher Bernard Stiegler argues: "The illusion of the triumph of the individual is fading. [...] Far from being characterised by the domination of individualism, this epoch turns out to be one of the herd-becoming of behaviour and of the generalised loss of individuation."[22]

I would rephrase this: since we are not allowed to subjectivise, arguably socialisation is blocked as well. That is, in order to connect us, and, through connecting us, we ultimately are isolated in our solipsistic but interchangeable datasets, and, from here, we are aggregated into a herd, a mass. The suffocation of the subjective inevitably also chokes the social.

At this juncture, a warning is in order: we psychoanalysts should proceed with utmost caution. If we think that our psychoanalytic models and theories can explain the vicissitudes of subjectivity and inter-subjectivity when they enter the digital, we should first and foremost acknowledge that the housing of subjectivity in the digital is precisely done on the basis of mainstream psychological models and theories.[23] That is, we should not fail to notice the psychologising armature of social media: the imperative to "share what you are thinking and how you feel" is handled by algorithms based on mainstream psychological models of thinking, emotions, and presence.

How should we as psychoanalysts deal with this, given that arguably the psychological models underlying these algorithms are not ours. Our understanding of the subjective (and the inter-subjective) is far removed from the current, hegemonic depictions of the human being: the cognitive, behaviouristic, neurobiological reductions of the human being. To fast-forward, if I argue that it are *the lies of psychology* what structure today's digital scene, then the central question is how does this function, how can a system that misinterprets subjectivity be so successful in capturing the attention of people, guiding and steering their behaviour and desires, aggregating and amassing them? To explain this phenomenon, we could argue that psychology itself is actually lacking when it comes to explaining the human, and this weakness harbours a different strength or power: that of making us *comply* with the categories of psychology. Let me explain myself: on the one hand, there is the already mentioned scientific interpellation: psychology tells us what we are, and this induces us to comply with the template offered to us. Although this mechanism actually draws its strength by enforcing us to adopt a detached position, that is we identify in the first place with the psychologists who tell us what and who we are. On the other hand, the digitalisation of subjectivity seems to involve a more direct steering and nudging: social media and the like peddle certain pre-configured contrived modes of being, of how to present oneself (e.g. through emoticons), and how to *be* with others. In this environment of pre-configured identities we are forced to assume pre-psychologised modes of (inter)-subjectivity, bypassing (albeit perhaps only in part) the scientific interpellation; the phony avatars and virtual environments have become today's new straitjackets.

This argument needs to be taken a step further. The lies of psychology underpinning the pre-configured identities work so well insofar as the truth of psychoanalysis is still structuring the situation. In the digital world psychology generates *fake subjectivities*, whilst "in reality" we are divided subjects, subjects of the unconscious, producing an array of symptoms when we embrace or succumb to the fake subjectivities forced upon us. Perhaps one could even argue that the lies of psychology are effective precisely because everyone knows the virtual world is phony and fake! Referring to the aforementioned passage in Freud's *Mass Psychology*, Adorno observes that most often people undergoing hypnosis remain somehow knowing that it is only a game:

> When the leaders become conscious of mass psychology and take it into their own hands, it ceases to exist in a certain sense. [...] Just as little as people believe in the depth of their hearts that the Jews are the devil, do they completely believe in their leader. They do not really identify themselves with him but act this identification, perform their own en-thusiasm, and thus participate in their leader's performance. [...] It is probably the suspicion of this fictitiousness of their own 'group psych-ology' which makes fascist crowds so merciless and unapproachable. If they would stop to reason for a second, the whole performance would go to pieces, and they would be left to panic.[24]

Or, transposed to our present-day ordeals, all too easily we adopt the bogus, pre-psychologised characters of the so-called "avatars" awaiting us in cyberspace, while ultimately keeping a certain reflective detachment, since we know very well that these entities are mere constructs representing a mirage of human psychology, a figment from which we remain detached. We are, after all, still subjects of modernity, that is, subjects of science, who look upon themselves from the perspective of science. As Adorno makes clear, it is precisely this reflective distance that allows us to play along, and enthusiastically act these identifications, knowing very well it is only a fictitious performance.

That said, we should ask whether Adorno's outline is fully transferable to our digital times. For, if the digital realm is prima facie egalitarian, in our case the authoritarian leader may still pop up, but just in a different guise.

For perhaps, in the virtual and digital habitat, the horizontal amassing of individuals according to profiles provided by psychology – bypassing or doing away with the leader – above all prepares for the return of masters and leaders in the real, analogue world. Simply put, being horizontally structured, the virtual and digital masses crave for real leaders. This is where we can see the rise of what Slavoj Žižek (2020) terms the "New Obscene Masters". Examples include Trump, Bolsonaro, Johnson, and Putin, among others. How does this come about? If for Freud the equality of all group members is based on a Leader figure – for whom baseline egalitarianism does not apply – Freud echoes the political theory that once society is grounded in law, that law must issue from a place beyond/before/outside itself.[25] This transgressive, perverse or even obscene "ground" of the law – exemplified by the Primal Father in Freud's understanding – in our times is no longer hidden but openly visible (where in a way, it is even better hidden), in what Žižek terms the "Obscene Masters".

This obscene litter of father figures are to my mind the cursed offspring of a capitalism that did away with hierarchical structures and has culminated in "digital surveillance capitalism", by which today's technology allows for allegedly direct and horizontal social inter-linking. Arguably, these new obscene father figures are mirroring the other "little father figures", those little leaders exemplified by such figures as Elon Musk and Mark Zuckerberg, who impose on their users a template of subject and social of their own design, and who rely on the hegemonic psychological models and theories to blueprint our digital lives and worlds. Freud notably pinpointed this exercise in mind-washing, contending that "mass psychology is the oldest psychology of the human race",[26] and eventually argues that this mass psychology is basically a derivate of the psychology of leadership: "Individual psychology must in fact be the same age as mass psychology, since from the outset there were two types of psychology: that of the individuals making up a mass and that of the father, the chief, the leader."[27]

The Primal Father's narcissistic psychological make-up "became the ground and reason for mass psychology".[28] This is also today's psychology, the mindset of the normal, well-adapted "ideal" individual: the psychology of what was one termed as the "Leading Success People". To each of us our inflated Ego, our restored Self – on Facebook, on Instagram, on Tik-Tok, on Linked-In, on Academia.edu – online we are all prime achievers. The occasional mental issues such as ADHD, ASD, hypersensitivity merely serve as ego boosters: tacked onto the banner of (neuro)diversity, these labels are worn as a badge of honour, confirming our narcissism and role as little leaders. However, as badges, these labels eventually suggest a minimal reflective distance from them: remember Adorno's fictitiousness here, we do not really identify with them but enact and perform our identification with them. Hence the ready-made psychological personalities offered to us by Musk, Zuckerberg and others are ultimately phony, and since underneath we realise it is all a sham, perhaps this is why we are tempted to turn to those bigger leader figures, the ones Freud refers to as "totally narcissistic, yet self-assured and independent".[29] Accordingly, figures like Trump lure the masses because of their untrammelled narcissism, compensating (by proxy) for our loss of Self, our withered identities, precisely as we are force-fed fake subjectivities constructed on the basis of the shallow and cardboardesque models of the ruling psychologies. It is this baseline of phoniness that people seek to transcend, indulging in dramatic performances, acting out to retrieve the yearned-for reality – which, however, is merely a chimera spoon-fed via digital echo-chambers – and from there we are coerced into joining the mob and taking to the streets, the kind of syndrome that led to the assault on the US Capitol, and similar performative expressions of behaviour.

At this point the inevitable question arises: what if, instead of the *lies* of psychology, we used the *truth* of psychoanalysis to underpin the digital realm: would that be the path to salvation, or instead open a Pandora's box? My question is whether psychoanalysis could chart and analyse the unintended and symptomatic outcomes of data technologies, and if so would it then be capable (in digital technologies, in algorithms) of mitigating the negative aspects of psychological profiling and data-aggregation? If so, should we then perhaps advise Berners Lee and his ilk in their attempts to re-democratise the world-wide-web and rescue it? That said, is there not also a case for vigilance, and the risk that this valuable knowledge would in turn be misused? Arguably, our insights might equally be employed to increase digital control. The upshot could be that the "obscene leaders" themselves could make effective use of psychoanalytically informed algorithms. It is anyone's guess whether the "truth" of psychoanalysis can prove itself more effective than the cheap psychologies piloting individuals amassed online.

At this point it might be opportune to reconsider the Lacanian dictum that psychoanalysis is not a *psychology*, and should not be generalized, but remain a science of the singular. By this, psychoanalysis does not offer a blueprint for modelling the virtual world and the myriad avatars populating it. Not a tool for steering the virtual masses. Freud's concepts such as the unconscious, the death drive, the polymorph perversity of sexuality, all point to a *subject*, that ultimately does not form a generalizable unit, equal to itself. In contrast, this subject – never a master of itself, always escaping itself, always at a distance from itself – brings to the fore a kind of subjectivity that structurally defies modelling or colonisation via algorithms. Freud's *Spaltung* – or for the Lacanians amongst us, the *barred subject* – could be reformulated as a *zero level of subjectivity*. In Žižek's words: "The subject is a basic constitutive void that drives subjectivation but which cannot ultimately be filled out by it."[30] It is precisely this constitutive destitution that, arguably, the digital and the algorithmic cannot model, it cannot handle a zero-level of subjectivity, for that would defy the reduction of the subject to metadata and to profiles, which are the basis of the aggregation process that amasses and ranks the public into discrete categories for profit.

In short, Freud's *unconscious* and Lacan's *objet a* (that which is defined by Lacan as the dual core of subjectivity: both lack and excess) cannot be digitalised as such. In this sense, when it comes to designing algorithms, psychoanalytical input is largely futile and useless but remains nevertheless useful when it comes to formulating a critique of the digitalisation of (inter) subjectivity. Psychoanalysis reveals how the fake psychologies underpinning the algorithmic amassing of people unwittingly get caught up in a different logic (unfathomable in the mainstream psychological models as such), a logic which psychoanalysis can lay bare, albeit a logic which itself cannot be digitalised or confined to an algorithm.[31] Ultimately, psychoanalysis is neither a psychology nor even a social psychology, it is a mass psychology: one which in the end envisions subjectivity and inter-subjectivity woven into something that defies the algorithm.

At this juncture, however, we reach yet another decisive issue: what if the digitalised lies of psychology suppress true subjectivity, that is, subjectivity as conceived by psychoanalysis, featuring "the subject of the unconsciousness", or to use even more Lacanian terms, "the subject of *objet a*"? The risk is relying too confidently in the human being's ability to elude the digital modelling and creatively find escape routes, even to take evasive action of a subversive nature. For, what if the digital technologies are increasingly apt to incorporate that creativity, even its subversive offshoots, and feed it all back into the digital economy? There, the digital would ultimately not fully capture the truth of subjectivity, but rather, it would simply make it impossible, leaving no breathing space whatsoever. Arguably, the digital technologies of today not only are structurally incapable of offering a space for the zero-level of subjectivity of psychoanalysis, but they also threaten to suffocate it entirely. Just consider how in digital culture being alone is increasingly impossible. Today, if you decide to go out alone, have a coffee in the afternoon (or a beer, a bit later in the afternoon), you might feel embarrassed or awkward at sitting there alone, so you reach for your little screen and scroll through your social network feeds. In this way, even a minor form of subjective destitution is voided, and while this type of incident once used to be a potential point of entry for the social, now there is no hiatus, we are permanently aggregated, amassed in the phoniness of the social network. Ironically, the most typical injunction of social media, *"share what you are thinking and how you feel"*, allows no leeway to withdraw, we are robbed of our not really knowing what we think, from our not knowing how we feel, if not, from our not feeling anything. Our little absences, where our thinking or our feelings escape ourselves, are turned into commodifiable presences.

The conundrum that the anti-social individualism of today's social media might mean the death-knell of the subject as we knew it, the subject of the unconscious, was already signalled in Apple's 1984 advertisement discussed higher. Apple's promotion of the personal computer leans on putting forward a superindividual not only fully in control of itself, but also fully independent from the group or the social as such. For psychoanalysis, in contrast, the subject constitutes itself precisely through the destitution of its alleged fully established individuality, through its own zero-level of subjectivity, through its being the subject of the unconscious, eventually disconnected from its own thinking and feelings. What Freud showed in his Mass Psychology is that is precisely there that subjectivity is always intertwined with sociality: the unconsciousness as *another scene* (Freud's "ein anderer Schauplatz") is also *the scene of the Other* (to put it in Lacanian). The major (but not unquestioned) premise of Mass Psychology is that this intertwinement inevitably is marked by the figure of the Leader. In the last chapter of Mass Psychology Freud links Oedipus to the myth of the Primal Father (as developed in Totem and Taboo) by sketching out the role of the hero-son. This favourite son of the mother who, as Freud hypothesis goes creates an epos in which the hero slays the Monster-Father, allowing each of us a narcissistic identification with this epic figure. The latter, which signals the return of the symbolic father, is Freud's final elaboration of his admonition that ultimately we cannot circumvent the Father or the Leader. The Apple heroine could be considered as an attempt to go for a non-patriarchal solution, smashing that what the son-poet once created, a story for each to follow, offering us thus an solipsistic alternative, that of the technology of the personal computer, allowing each of us to create our own epos.

When all is said and done, it is my opinion that digital technologies tend to push us toward an acting out and resurrecting new Totems, namely the new figures of the Obscene Fathers. Perhaps the Apple heroine signals a false feminisation, a fake genderisation that stands for the "soft" emotions, the affect, things bodily, all aspects that are stressed in the mainstream psychological sciences as the main features – if not assets – of the human individual. There, becoming the quantifiable, chartable, digitisable and hence commodifiable *genderised human*, the quest can start new Father-Leader Totems.

Hence, looking once again at Apple's launch advertisement and the anonymous audience the heroine passes down the aisle on her way to smash the screen, I see a certain heterogeneity: they are not actually in uniform but in rags – suggesting perhaps the destitute *Lumpenproletariat*. Not all in the audience has a shaved head, there is plenty of diversity, there are a mixture old and young (some of them are even wearing something that could be an oxygen mask, signalling disability or sickness?). Just before the woman's hammer hits the screen, we see a little boy in the crowd. This image prompts me to return to my youth-movement days and identify with him. And in my mind's eye I image someone stretching out their leg to trip the heroine, dirtying her fake immaculate white tank-top, ruining here all-too-perfect hairdo, her abominable uniform… Maybe the hammer has already been launched through the air – so much for the better. But now she is on the floor, her robotic components scattered down the aisle. Would that alternative vision herald a more emancipatory, revolutionary and collective future, perhaps with different technologies than those we have today? Who can tell, but I for one am thrilled at the prospect.

Notes

1   This talk is based on my presentation with more or less the same title (The Truths of Psychoanalysis: Defying the Lies of Psychology that Fuel the Amassing of Individuals) for the conference "Thoughts for the times on groups and masses" organised by the Sigmund Freud Museum of Vienna, June 10–11, 2022, Vienna, Austria.

2   https://www.freud-museum.at/en/detail/on-groups-and-masses (accessed 08-11-2023).

3   S. Freud, 'Mass Psychology and Analysis of the "I"' (1921), in: *Mass Psychology and Other Writings*, ed. J. A. Underwood. London. Penguin Books, 2004, pp. 15-100. Freud's text is abbreviated to '*Mass Psychology*' in the following.

4   T. W. Adorno, 'Freudian Theory and the Pattern of Fascist Propaganda', in: *The Culture Industry: Selected Essays on Mass Culture*, ed. J. M. Bernstein, London: Routledge, 1991, pp. 115-135, p. 121.

5   Freud, *Mass Psychology*, p. 76.
6   Ibid., p. 81.
7   J. Lacan, 'British Psychiatry and the War', in: *Psychoanalytical Notebooks of the London Circle* 4, ([1947] 2000).
8   For a still broader discussion, see J. De Vos, 'Psychoanalysis, a Psychology of the Masses for These Digital Times', in: *Psychotherapy and Politics International* 19/3 (2021): e1597.
9   S. Freud, *Mass Psychology*, p. 95.
10 I am alluding here to the concept "interpellation" of Louis Althusser, L. Althusser, 'Ideology and Ideological State Apparatuses (Notes Towards an Investigation)', in: *Lenin and Philosophy and Other Essays*. London: New Left Books, 1971.
11 https://encyclopedievlaamsebeweging.be/nl/jeugdbeweging (accessed 08-11-2023).
12 Romanticism was already influential in the 19th century in youth circles in Germany.
13 S. Freud, M*ass Psychology*, p. 65.
14 J. De Vos, *Psychologisation in Times of Globalisation*. London: Routledge, 2012; J. De Vos, *The Metamorphoses of the Brain. Neurologization and Its Discontents*, New York: Palgrave Macmillan, 2016.
15 S. Freud, *Mass Psychology*, p. 75.
16 T. W. Adorno, 'Freudian Theory and the Pattern of Fascist Propaganda', p. 132.
17 J. Lacan, 'British Psychiatry and the War', pp. 9-34, p. 11.
18 https://www.freud-museum.at/en/detail/on-groups-and-masses (accessed 08-11-2023).
19 N. Braunstein, 'La pandemia y la psicología de las masas', in: *Psicoanalítica* 10 (2020). https://psicoanalitica.uv.mx/index.php/Psicoanalitica/article/view/2571 (accessed 08-11-2023).
20 https://www.youtube.com/watch?v=ErwS24cBZPc (accessed 08-11-2023).
21 A. Hern, 'Tim Berners-Lee on 30 years of the world wide web: "We can get the web we want"', in: *The Guardian* 2019. https://www.theguardian.com/technology/2019/mar/12/tim-berners-lee-on-30-years-of-the-web-if-we-dream-a-little-we-can-get-the-web-we-want (accessed 08-11-2023).
22 B. Stiegler, 'Suffocated Desire, or How the Culture Industry Destroys the Individual: Contribution to a Theory of Mass Consumption', in: *Parrhesia: A Journal of Critical Philosophy* 13 (2011), pp. 52-61, p. 54.
23 For further discussion, see J. De Vos, *The Digitalisation of (Inter) Subjectivity: A Psycritique of the Digital Death Drive*. London: Routledge, 2020.
24 T. W. Adorno, 'Freudian Theory and the Pattern of Fascist Propaganda', pp. 136-137.
25 See for example the theories of Carl Schmitt discussed by Giorgio Agamben, *Homo sacer*, D. Heller-Roazen (Transl.). Stanford, CA.: Stanford University Press, 1998.
26 Freud, *Mass Psychology*, p. 101.
27 Ibid., p. 102.
28 Ibid.
29 Ibid.

[30] S. Žižek & G. Daly, *Conversations with Žižek*. Cambridge: Polity Press, 2004, p. 4.

[31] For an extended argumentation of this line of thought, see J. De Vos, 'Fake subjectivities: Interpassivity from (Neuro) Psychologization to Digitalization', in: *Continental Thought & Theory: A Journal of Intellectual Freedom* 2/1 (2018), pp. 5-31.

Representing the Crisis of Representation

Giuseppina Antinucci

Introduction

Centenaries are not mere temporal events, they can also constitute veritable *lieux de mémoire* that instigate renewed reflection and, in the case of the Freudian oeuvre, occasion the task of textual re-reading and glossing. The century elapsed since Sigmund Freud's *Massenpsychologie* was first published, has witnessed societal phenomena that have accrued in an unquestionable anthropological shift, whose existential import is substantial. Consequently, as it is true of authentic classics – as Italo Calvino argues – *Massenpsychologie* prompts a revisitation of the text with the aim of furthering its resonances and offering conceptual tools to analyse our contemporaneity. In particular, the intersecting axes of the vertical relationship to the leader, and the horizontal fraternal component, feature as two itineraries leading to diverse identificatory processes, the former induces passivation and erotised subjection to the leader's paternal authority, whilst the latter promotes identification en masse with the similar-but-different-other that is the sibling.

Rosine Perelberg[1] differentiates between the murder of the despotic, perverse, narcissistic father – necessary to institute the civilised order – and the dead father, namely, the psychic structure which founds the symbolic order or the Lacanian "Name of the Father". The work of mourning undergirds these processes and is crucial for internalising the symbolic authority over a societal jurisdiction worthy of collective investment, guaranteed by the metapsychic, metasocial "Law and Language", which promotes the work of representation in its twofold meaning, psychic and political. In this sense *Massenpsychologie*, harking back to Freud's *Totem and Taboo* and foreshadowing *Civilisation and Its Discontents*, inaugurates the anthropologically informed psychoanalytic discourse that compounds the theoretical scaffolding to inquire into subjectivities imbedded in history – rather than prehistory – where identification, with its varieties and trajectories, is a pivotal concept to

123

Giuseppina Antinucci

examine the psychic structuring of the world of cultural objects. Essentially, I propose a structural interpretation of the three texts, to render the transitional work of bridging internal and external realities. As Freud himself suggests, individual and group psychology are two vertices to investigate the same phenomena from complementary perspectives.

> It is true that individual psychology is concerned with the individual man and explores the paths by which he seeks satisfaction for his instinctual impulses; but only rarely and under certain exceptional conditions is individual psychology in a position to disregard the relations of this individual to others.[2]

How to think about ideals, conflicts, desires, anxieties, defences, ethics; namely, how *Kultur* is pre-consciously and unconsciously deposited through syntonic and/or interdicted modalities and objects of identification? Winnicott's transitional space of culture proves to be heuristically judicious, for it is construed as the space we inhabit, where we create/find objects, in developmental continuity with its infantile precursor, in the paradoxical locus wherein self and non-self coexist.

Trajectories of Identification in Digitalised Culture

A consistent concern with the multifarious vicissitudes of identification features in Freud's works since his *Studies on Hysteria*, includes the pre-psychoanalytic *Project*, and increasingly gains significance as not merely "one psychical mechanism among others, but the operation itself whereby the human subject is constituted."[3] The *fil rouge* of these conceptualisations is how the subject deals with loss, whether experienced and signified as object loss or loss of (parts of) self. As a primary articulation of this psychical narrative, the Oedipus complex is the systematic rendition of the vicissitudes of identification throughout the variations of the Freudian models of the mind. Principally the structural model, however, and the formulation of the psychic agencies, alongside the study of narcissism, nuances the trajectories of identification in their archaic, defensive and/or structuring function, imbued with oedipal and pre-oedipal ties and unconscious fantasies. *Massenpsychologie* is situated in the temporal arch of the transition to the second topography, which interrogates the shadow(s) that lost objects cast upon the ego, and adumbrates the role played by the early attachment to the mother, which can account for the regression or fixation to the fascination, dependence, and erotised passivation that Freud observes in unstructured groups of the mass society. Freud's observations refer to how individuals behave and function in groups: they project both their lost narcissism as ego-ideal and their moral agency, their superego; they regress formally and topically when they think per images, and their employment of secondary and primary identifications provides the vertex to investigate cross-identifications. If there is such a thing as a "group of two", the group mentality is construed as an unconscious assemblage of the psyche that permits us to hypothesise what goes on intra-psychically, intersubjectively, and trans-generationally.

In 1921 Freud was still unaware of the momentous texture of the infant's pre-oedipal attachment to the mother; it is, in fact, that early bond that imbues primary identification with its jouissance for mother and baby alike. Consequently, the undifferentiated nucleus in each of us pertains to the unconscious primordial group mentality, informed by that early trace. *Group Psychology and the Analysis of the Ego* could also be read as foreshadowing the psychic functioning of the group of two of mother and baby, considered from the perspective of primary identification, which will be furthered by Donald W. Winnicott, Wilfred Bion, José Bleger, and Thomas Ogden. Bleger names "agglutinated core" the undifferentiated nucleus wherein identity is rooted: an *institutionalized self* that is essentially nested in a phantasmatic maternal somato-psyche, whose jouissance, vicissitudes and (homo)sexuality it partakes.

Thus epistemologically contoured, the concept of identity has increasingly garnered psychoanalytic attention, due to the task of formulating diagnostics and treatment for the presentation of contemporary malaise, often clustered under the umbrella of *failure of the work of subjectivation*. When regarding the work of subjectivation as a process imbued with the work of culture, psychoanalysis is put to work to address the malaise and psychic functioning of the digitalised world, whose spatial coordinates are rapidly shifting and ever more delocalised, and its instantaneous temporality is the corollary of the dominant "regime of presentism."[4] Furthermore, the concept of primary identification is heuristically expedient to inquire into the clinical states of depression and panic, where failure in differentiation and individuation are salient features and signal the problematics of oedipal structuring, whose destiny would ordinarily be secondary identification. Fear of breakdown prompts the request of therapeutic help, often formulated as critically urgent by patients who feel *lost*, and *all over the place*. Poor subjectivation and self-object differentiation, failure of separation-individuation characterises this clinical picture, pointing to psychic functioning within the "core position",

125

symbiotic and ambiguous,[5] similarly described by Ogden as "autistic-contiguous position",[6] where identification is tinged with a tenaciously insistent hold on the primary object. Time and again, young adults enter our consulting rooms which, in their confusion and need, they phantasmatically envision as an A&E department, and clamour that their terror of breaking down be ameliorated by a "double-click",[7] whilst phobically rejecting the toil of thinking, which they construe as incompatible with *presentism*. This presentation reveals that the *third space* to function symbolically, is yet to be constituted.

Winnicott judiciously interpolates the attribute *maternal* between *primary* and *identification*, to address the contribution of the mother's care and synthetic function the baby internalises as s/he emerges from the symbiotic unit. Essential is the mother's somato-psychic responsiveness to her infant's needs, sourced by her capacity to identify with her baby – and her own infantile self – to enter an envelope of empathic attunement before and beyond words. Laplanche speaks of the mother's *seduction* through ministering body care to her new-born, thereby inaugurating the *general anthropological situation* and initiation of psychic birth.[8] The word seduction addresses the exchange of pleasurable amorous gaze of the beginning stages, but also broadly delineates and signifies the sphere of intimacy, which always alludes to something more, something further, namely, the unconsciously codified trace which sources all experiences of intimacy.

My engagement with Infant Observation has alerted me to the ubiquitous presence of electronic devices which speak for an increasingly extensive recourse to the applications entrusted to provide ready-made *solutions* to parental anxieties and desires. Mothers seek from their iPhone answers to questions about infant care, physical exercises, educational toys: this shift towards predominant managerial style is a far cry from Winnicott's maternal preoccupation. The all-knowing device, to which submission is demanded, is commended to deliver an ideal mother-baby image, sourced in the woman's self-ideal(isation), whilst in the affectively embodied encounter, the screen is positioned between mother and baby in lieu of a permeable intrapsychic and intersubjective contact barrier and ultimately serves as a defensive screen to protect her from the emotional impact of the *infantile* helplessness in herself, roused by her in-fant.

From the baby's vertex, who and what is the omniscient all-powerful object, always already there? The device is present(ed) rather than represented, thereby introducing an early triangulation with a disembodied entity that assuages mother's anxiety, whilst enigmatically signifying her desire. Will it be construed *après-coup* as a prosthetic-phallic quality of the mother and radical repudiation of her femaleness, that very form of *being* Winnicott locates in the psyche of both sexes? Freud had already hypothesized how the horror of passivity vis-à-vis the maternal imago constitutes the bedrock of the psyche. Will the early triangulation promote in the infant the identification with a phallic-ness lodged in a dissociated silo in permanent disjunction from the "pure" femaleness of being?[9] Further questions pertain to the *sexual*: how do babies translate the enigma of the idiosyncratic digital object of the parents' desire? What is the psychic status of that "other of the object"[10] when it is a technological implement? How and where do infants position themselves in the mother's or father's erotics, when triangulated by a screen?

Feminist and cultural studies suggest that digital objects are psychically processed as enigmatic, and captured by the *sexual*, albeit differently from analogues. There are echoes of this formulation in Stephen Hartman, who postulates that, the Unconscious being a system open to external influences, analogic and digital objects are introjected and influence each other in structure and content. Following Laplanche (1997), Hartman maintains that technology *implants* objects in our psyche, as unwittingly

> [...] technology penetrates the unconscious with a foreign digital lexicon and temporality that always already lurks as an Other in one's own burgeoning idiom. Thus, nascent cyberobjects trade among erotic objects carrying with them inherited enigmas of their technological birth.[11]

Hartmann proposes a critique of identification, to be replaced – he claims – by that of introjection, revisited and interpreted as a process that prescinds from the temporal past-ness and embodied presence of the object, whose likeness is the terrain of identification. It would appear that different objects are introjected like separate dialects, but it is not so clear – I argue – whether and in what contexts they might interact and commingle, or whether their diverse lexicon requires different translations and follow different itineraries. The dual track hypothetically designated for digital and analogic objects remains to be tested in the consulting room, bearing in mind that the psychoanalytic object par excellence is an embodied person, with an internal world which enigmatically sources the infant's interpellations. The quest: "What do you want from me?" generates theories and fantasies, not easily subsumed under the register of mastery.

Further interrogations concerning development, internalisation, introjection, and identification with enigmatic devices have implications for the study of the ever-increasing phenomena of de-subjectivation and disturbance of identity, signalling the failure of the oedipal structuring and secondary identifications. Psychoanalytic discourse founds psychic life on primary identification with the nurturing mother – which shapes the development of object relationships and mature identifications – as grounding of a sound ontological ecology, where psyche-soma compounds a unit. It is axiomatic that, if the amorous mutual gaze is wanting, no object can be lost or renounced, rather the fixity of the ideal and the promise of "loss-less-ness"[12] takes its place as illusory creation outside the psychic field.

When encountering the brittle subjectivity exposed to the fascination of illusions, the psychoanalyst's remit consists primarily in instantiating the space where differences can be thought between inner and shared spatio-temporal reality, dream, fantasy and daydream, self and other that, once discovered in its radical otherness, can be located outside the specular domain.

Demise of the Symbolic Order

Clinical thought needs the underpinning of the concept of *Kulturarbeit* to contextualise generalised forms of malaise. Freud based the work of culture on the repression of drive satisfaction that each generation accomplishes and unconsciously transmits to the next in the form of ego-ideal and superego, which demand similar work of repression and identification with values, norms, ideals, and with the forefathers. Achievement of the symbolic pact is predicated upon impulse renunciation, and is constitutive of the polity; furthermore it is implemented by the transformation of violence into social bond with fellow citizens, to secure viable existential conditions for the majority.

The current crisis of the symbolic pact denotes a failure of the work of culture, and undergirds the ideals of a triumphant individual, master of his/her world, successful inasmuch as s/he expunges any trace of vulnerability and suffering, construed as weakness. Its corollary is a crisis of the investment in representativity and representational procedures within the body politic and the internal world alike, which impacts the subject's inner dialogue. The technological turn has contributed to fashion a cultural environment whose mandate is to perform according to the phallic on/off logic of operational machinery. Additionally, the *cri de cœur* concerning the crisis of representation comes from allied disciplines which connote the present as a culture of trauma, marked by the wound inflicted to the symbolic order by massive exterminations and genocides which remain unmourned, and impact the collective memory and the symbolic representation of the unlanguaged. Failure of the mourning work results in the defensive sado-masochistic impasse characteristic of borderline and narcissistic character organizations, which seemingly have become cultural traits too and put to work the psychoanalytic perspective on contemporaneity.

Amber Jacobs (2015) proposes a psychosocial analysis of the technological imaginary: she claims that the analogical photographic image depends on the presence of the object, both in the shape of the camera shutter opening and closing, and the development of the negative in the darkroom, where the exposure leaves a mark signifying absence. Conversely, the digital image has no reference to material presence, thanks to its pixelated existence. Jacobs bases on her analysis of digital production a critique of the psychoanalytic "navel logic",[13] founded on the presence of the object to be represented after its loss. If there is no presence or present-ness, she concludes, there can only be loss-less-ness; therefore psychoanalysis, with its conceptual armoury of primal scene and mourning work is an obsolete conceptual apparatus. Jacobs engages with the psychoanalytic discourse and avows that one part of our mind still functions analogically, hence a multidisciplinary conversation is fruitful, but psychoanalysis should no longer posit questions regarding origins, when faced with the digital native's quest: Who and what am I? Who and what will I be? This line of argument discreetly erases the temporal *past-ness* constructed in the *après-coup* of the heterochronia of psychoanalysis, which is not an essential datum, and the object's presence is merely a function of memory, desire, dream, and fantasy. Moreover, deleting history from the register of temporalities does not exempt the subject from their need to inscribe their biography into a narrative of origins, even when parentage is replaced by phantasmatic parthenogenesis. If the navel link with the maternal body and the past is defensively scotomized, is the elected futurity of the oracular address to a cyber-dispenser of identity definitions like "digital native", more advantageous? But what of the unconscious, and of its irreducible dimension of otherness? In the unconsciously powered ontological narrative, the object's presence or absence makes a difference anyhow, and so to suffering.

The hypothetical dual track for internalising digital and analogic objects is convincing, as is the proposal that all enigmatic objects solicit the work of translation and can be captured by the sexual – or, conversely, be sequestered by omnipotent destructiveness.

Similarly, Hartman proposes that digital objects enter the consulting room as distinct from the analogic ones, each available for diverse uses and functions, such as reformulating the pain of loss, morphed into cybermourning, where "the emphasis is not on reparation to the loss but on transforming the structure of experience"[14], because,

> [a]s modern culture shifts toward ever-greater elasticity of object-related experience in collective space, the priority on object-loss shifts toward immortality. As such, collective loss online is a very different species of loss from the kinds of losses that humans, who individually group into collectivities, share. Our lost objects *gain* immortality in collective space. I am not arguing that losses need no longer be suffered, but that that suffering is increasingly mitigated and reconstituted by *mourning's* sudden twin: 'cybermourning'.[15]

Incontestably our psyche is heterogeneous, and we are inhabited by a plurality of aspects imbued with affectively connoted experiences, memories and relationships; the *Spaltung* of the ego whereby the same object can solicit a "yes" or "no" enunciation of reality is a psychotic defence potentially available to everyone; however, it is a matter of degree whether it pervades most of the psyche, severing its link with reality, or is framed by wish and illusion. Whilst it is essential to study the psychical rendering of digital objects, and their coalescence into internal structures, it is also undeniable that the ideological use of these studies is problematic, as it is highly complex that the given-ness of the body is questioned, and frequently psychoanalysis is discarded through a disingenuous recourse to the strawman logic, such as: *classical psychoanalysis is underpinned by the concept of present-ness, which is obsolete, hence we modern can dispense with the psychic pain of the mourning work.* This argumentum is epistemologically tendentious, and clinically unfounded, especially when the clinician is faced with an ever-increasing incidence of hypochondriasis and psycho-somatic decompensation among adolescents and young adults. Perhaps here the body becomes the site of an insoluble quandary: as the object of fantasised mastery – and repository of aggression when repudiated – it is fated to return, violently morphed into the excesses of persecutory anxieties and paranoia. Maybe cyberspace reveals a collective cultural dysmorphia, which demands to be critically deconstructed, rather than celebrated. Still, the epistemology of cyberculture continues to constitute a challenging navigation, between the Scylla of condemnation and the Charybdis of enthusiasm, whereby it is essential to maintain focus on the intricacies and the unknown-ness of the human subject.

An outlook on the informatics civilization inscribed within the faltering symbolic guarantors – whose function is the structuring of the psyche – raises questions pertaining to the trajectories of the internalisation of its mandates conveyed through paradigmatic and enigmatic devices. The prosthetic God vaunts a seamlessly efficient omnipotence that global citizens unconsciously absorb as ideal, whilst projecting their fantasies, which come back as real or hyper-real. The image of the Almighty defensively scotomises human beings' terror and helplessness in the face of uncontrollable natural events, dangerous conflicts with strangers, and the fear of death – all of which the *Kulturarbeit* should to some degree buffer and symbolically bind. The unconscious pact between the subject and the social order becomes the locus of psycho-social malaise when the symbolic order presents features of the primitive narcissistic father of the primal horde. Necessarily, only dialectical reasoning can grasp the internal – external dynamics by shedding light on the flow of projection and introjection. We have created our world, whist also the world is in us, and traverses us in ways that is essential to interrogate, problematize and think, notwithstanding the cultural ideal of acting without thinking, as the philosopher Günther Anders maintains, when he regards the technological turn as an anthropological shift, whereby the subject functions according to the modality "if it can be done, it must be done",[16] and such operationalism forecloses the space and time for imaginative elaboration and thought.

> It is not enough to change the world. That is all we have ever done. That happens even without us. We also have to interpret this change. And precisely in order to change it. So that the world will not go on changing without us. And so that it is not changed in the end into a world without us.[17]

This is a veritable "technocracy" – the philosopher suggests – in the sense that history unfolds within the regime of technology as co-historical agent alongside human beings. Anders contends that a *Promethean disjunction* characterises the anthropology of the technocratic era, whose distinctive feature is the collective fantasy of omnipotence of action to the detriment of imagination and thought, thereupon the "prosthetic God"[18] emerges as a culturally syntonic fetishised ideal. Ironic epitome of this confusion of tongues, the adjective "virtual" that Freud employed as the constitutive attribute of psychic life, has been sequestered as an adjunct to "reality", with the resulting hypostatisation of the domain of intuition, imagination, and symbolic thought: the hyper-reality of hyper-modernity reifies and flattens representational imagination, contributing to a veritable impoverishment of inner life. Nonetheless, the flipside of the omnipotent fantasy is the *Promethean shame* which presently haunts subjectivities. Turkle advances an analogous argument when she deconstructs the teleological myth of ethically neutral progress and writes: "Technologies are never 'just tools'"[19], in agreement with Malater, who names them "evocative objects" that cause us to see ourselves and our world differently.[20] Both authors reprise Bollas's formulation of evocative objects, that exist in the cultural world and are fitting to articulate our personal idiom.

Catching the drift of my young patient's narratives, I witness their attempts to construct their interactive identities, through the creation of a plurality of selves, to stage plays of anticipation of movements towards relationships in a cyber-transitional space, which might equally become a sidereal site inhabited by simulacra, a place to abscond to, so as not to be found. If this quandary is brought into the treatment, the analytic relationship can offer the possibility to initialise the ontological ecology so conspicuously lacking in the broader symbolic environment. The analyst's embodied presence is crucial, as long as s/he maintains an unobtrusive stance to allow the patient to identify with a thinking mind, tasked to differentiate temporalities, spaces, inner and outer domains, until the ego can rely on its own stable nucleus, which constitute the sole guarantee of the object's optimal distance: neither engulfing, nor abandoning. Internalisation and identification are rooted in the registration and mnemic traces of early sensory contact. Therefore "the role of the body's reception and participation in the unlanguaged"[21] becomes the locus of the interpersonal being-with-the-other and traces a trajectory for the quality of autoeroticism and its integrative or split off, disavowed destiny. When not timely caught by the therapeutic couch, might the young subject sojourn in an anxiety-ridden locality of the "autistic-contiguous position"[22] which grounds him/her primarily in sensuous mode of intermittent – and interacting – existence? What sort of evocative immersive objects would they finally rich out to, in cyberspace?

> To be immersed in cyberspace is to be thrown into a set of paradoxes. But when entering cyberspace we are within a kind of dreamscape that still operates as if it were reality. To be caught **in** the gaze of cyberspace is to be subject to forms of identification and interpellation that only operate insofar as we know that we are subjects surfing cyberspace; to be hit by the real *in* cyberspace – at moments of shock that break the illusion of self-sufficient representation structured by the software-is

but a moment of disturbance that we know will be 'sutured', that the phantasmatic frame will be repaired. Cyberspace is bound-aried by the process of logging in and out, such that we expect that the narrative at one part of the communication broken at one moment will be restored at the next.[23]

A compelling feature of informatics is its promise of a "celestial world of loss-less-ness"[24] to the digital subject, who, in turn, projects onto the screen the unconscious fantasy of inhabiting a desirable "elsewhere", which renders them invulnerable to pain, separation, loss, grief and whatsoever, inevitable, renunciation. In the "group of two" of the digital subject and his/her screen, the virtual domain of the possible and the boundaried real are confused with omnipotent wishes and fantasies, in the privacy of the mediat(is)ed "cloud" with its alluringly illusory mastery of the object-world.[25]

As concluding remarks, the psychoanalytic discourse poses multilayered questions which pertain to the sources of fascination with a fictive self-idea(l) that risks collapsing into confusion, at the very junction where the boundaries between the inner and outer worlds are blurred.

A View from the Analytic Room

An excerpt from the treatment of a first-year university student aptly epitomises the cyber-inflected normalisation of a mode of functioning which denies generational and sexual differences. The attendant confusion exposes the problematic of the demise of the symbolic order and the predicaments it engenders.

The safely familiar world of Eloisa's childhood imploded just as she was looking forward to going to university when, on the eve of her Baccalaureate, her father announced that he would soon leave home, because he had met another woman and was in love with her. Eloisa's mother reacted with stupefied paralysis and became severely depressed, and Eloisa and her younger brother had to quickly learn how to manage the family home. Initially she expressed her hurt and rage by repudiating her father, whom she refused to see: disoriented and uncertain, she felt she had lost her position of father's favourite, having become cognisant of the presence of a rival. An outlet for her anger and secretly revengeful wish to humiliate her father became available when the parents asked her to act as their intermediary, whereupon she intimated that he should renounce his affair and return to his wife. But during the summer Eloisa's symptomatology began to interfere with her psychosomatic wellbeing and capacity to attend to her academic work, and she decided to seek outside help. I encountered a very anxious, sad, lost and somewhat rigid young woman who could not settle into her new life at university and make new friends. Neither could she return home, which had become the site of a shambolic paternal crisis; she found a solution to her predicament by filling up her time with obsessive ideas and compulsive online access to Facebook to check what her father was doing, since he featured among her Facebook 'friends'. Surreptitiously, through her father's account, Eloisa accessed his lover's profile, and discovered that the aging gentleman, who had sworn he would break off the liaison with his young mistress – slightly older than his daughter – in reality was lying. The photos her rival posted on Facebook, in fact, together with her "engaged" status, became for Eloisa the testimonial evidence that her father's word was but a lie-speech, and that he was the cavalier manufacturer of fake news. The man was eventually exposed for who he was. Also, to her dismay, her repressed fantasy of being the oedipal victor had violently surfaced: she felt overwhelmed, profoundly troubled, and confused. At this stage, my work with the analysand essentially aimed at addressing her confusion, thereby disentangling her unconscious fantasy from the reality of her father's affair with someone young enough to be his daughter. Whose return of the repressed were we witnessing? The generational symmetry was driving Eloisa to self-destruction. If this was a psychic area dominated by unstructured unconscious material, it could be argued that the analytic process instituted a structuring function, which resulted in a disquieting dream:

> I dreamt that I was in my parents' bed – I am not sure whether I was a child or my age. I was attracted to both my mum and dad but wanted to keep them apart and I began to kiss my dad in the mouth. I woke up feeling overwhelmed by anxiety and disgust – I just wanted to throw up, to rid myself of those repugnant images. Where did they come from?

Morphing the images into a narrative to address a receptive and signifying Other/analyst provided much needed relief for Eloisa, whose dream emerged as a subjective epiphany contoured by an enhanced sense of conviction regarding our work: she was experiencing and recovering/constructing her "memories in feelings."[26] The intensive analytic engagement afforded Eloisa the subjectivising link necessary to unfold the task of identity and psychic restructuring, which culminated in her successful PhD application to an overseas university.

Eloisa's case substantiates a twofold line of inquiry about subjectivities on the cusp of history, where the psychopathology presented by the patient and her family finds resonance with the gamut of possibilities offered or sanctioned by a given culture. On one level, the patient who unveils the truth by interrogating Facebook appears to be the modern seeker of an oracular pronouncement, burdened by the attendant anxieties and fantasies; on another level, the young woman seems to claim her filial entitlement to triumphantly and omnipotently access the thalamus secrets of a phantasmatic transgressive couple. Voyeuristic intrusion and involvement in the primal scene are enabled by technology – if I can, I will! However, through her actions, she becomes the privileged witness of a virtual and perverse primal scene, which overwhelms her with anxiety and guilt: in the absence of any oedipal prohibition, the secret is enticing and represents an invitation to transgress the civilising oedipal law, instituted by the taboos of incest and murder. Eloisa situates Facebook in the place of the Other always already supposed to know: she appears to submit to such an omniscient entity unquestioningly, as a matter of fact, and acts unthinkingly, while she unconsciously identifies with her idealised image of a prosthetic God, which defends her from the pain of becoming fully aware of the failure of the paternal function in her psyche, and her shame for feeling abandoned. If anything, Facebook constitutes the split-off locality where a collusive and confusing intergenerational encounter occurs, indicative of a pathological group organisation along *incestual* lines.

Racamier advances the hypothesis that the *incestuel* is a specific register and mode of family functioning, marked by the lack of transformation of incest into an unconscious fantasy destined to be repressed. Even if it does not go so far as real sexual enactment, the *incestuel* occupies a fixed position between oedipal structuring and incest as a real event: it is rather a relational cocoon, where incest remains an open possibility, un-elaborated, un-mourned, un-repressed. In Eloisa's family the *incestuel* is revealed and staged in the split-off theatre of Facebook. Unsurprisingly the chosen denotation "friendship" obfuscates the specificity of the bond of kinship; on the contrary, its mystifying associations gesture to the field of legitimate exogamic *liaisons*. Because technologies are never mere tools, neither is it the Facebook-object that evocatively articulates and reveals the *incestuel*, as a register of family functioning that can occasion psychopathological manifestations and enactments because *friendship* between familial generations is normalised as a desirable cultural trait, until its anti-oedipal meaning is exposed by psychic suffering. When critically interrogated and interpreted psychoanalytically, this normalising symmetry shows its darker shadow, because, as Racamier affirms:

> [W]here Oedipus is well-established, there is no place for the *incestuel*. We must also remember that the Oedipus complex is not a mere complex located in the unconscious; we know that it is an organizer of individual, family and social life, through the provision of structure and perspectives [...] The Oedipus complex takes shape as a *perspective* between conscious and unconscious, between fantasy and action, like a narrative whose origin is drawn on the twofold evidence (conscious and unconscious, individual and family) of the difference between the sexes and the generations.[27]

The analysis helped Eloisa to differentiate fantasy, dream, action, sexes, and generations, thus establishing the Oedipus complex and, hopefully, in time repression might emerge and open for her new vistas where symbolic bisexual identifications might result in creative pursuits and pleasures. The analyst is not there to trace or predict her patient's libidinal vicissitudes, elaboration, and destiny. But to return to our contemporary technologically inflected discourse, Eloisa's case sheds light both on the subject's suffering and on the global defensive normalization of what is a demise, rather, a perverse turn of the symbolic order, evinced in the ego-ideal and superego psychopathology across the generations, where the anti-Oedipus interferes with secondary identifications. Moreover, the case lends itself to be inscribed in the broader field of sexual morality and ethics, namely, the Freudian Civilization which informs the cultural superego and is transmitted trans-generationally. Indeed in Eloisa's family the intrapsychic, interpersonal, and transgenerational (transpersonal level) are intermingled, and render manifest the unconscious mandate to transgress the Oedipal order of the chain of generations. After all, her father's displaced incestuous enactment reveals his transgression of the Oedipal interdict, hence, he cannot function as a symbolic guarantor. If anything, he failed in his exercise of transformatively carrying the carnality of his daughter's desire into the field of speech. How could he, if he was the one who introduced her to the lie-speech, thus perverting the symbolic order? Does this instance not evoke the crime committed by Laius, when he abrogated the responsibility of occupying his paternal position, and, in *loco parentis,* seduced his friend's son Chrysippus, and later repudiated fathering his own child? When repression no longer holds across the generations, the ripple effect is the breaking down of the symbolic pact between parents and children, whose isomorphism recalls the social contract. Parental disavowal of the temporal order and premonition of their own mortality, due to their intense castration and separation anxieties, can ensue in failure to inscribe their own biography in the generational sequence. They transmit or project their difficulties onto their offspring, as defensive nuclei that cannot be explicitly addressed and worked through, but enhance vulnerability to psychopathology. In a sense, the mirage of loss-less-ness configures a nostalgic phantasmatic paradise for everyone which renders the generations illusorily and collusively symmetrical, partaking a form of malaise, in which "they are all in it together", unfortunately with little consolation. The psychoanalyst is tasked with the job of thinking, at times under fire, to offer hospitality and containment to suffering wanderers, seeking a psychic home where to safely experience the malaise of civilization.

Notes

1   R. Perelberg, *Murdered Father, Dead Father*. London: Routledge 2015.
2   S. Freud, *Group Psychology and the Analysis of the Ego* (1921), *SE* 18, pp. 65-144, p. 69.
3   J. Laplanche & J.-B. Pontalis, *The Language of Psychoanalysis*. London; Hogarth, 1973, p. 206.
4   F. Hartog, 'Encounters with Chronos, 1970–2020'. Paper presented at the Symposium "The experience of time", 7–8 April 2022, unpublished.
5   *José Bleger. Symbiosis and Ambiguity. A Psychoanalytic Study*, J. Churcher & L. Bleger (Eds.). London: Routledge, 2012.
6   T. Ogden, *The Primitive Edge of Experience*. Lanham, ML: Jason Aronson, 1989.
7   Bruno Latour, 2022: https://www.franceculture.fr/emissions/les-chemins-de-la-philosophie/les-chemins-de-la-philosophie-du-lundi-21-mars-2022 (accessed 22-02-2023).
8   J. Laplanche, 'The theory of Seduction and the Problem of the Other', in: *The International Journal of Psychoanalysis* 78/4, pp. 653-666 (1997).
9   D. W. Winnicott, 'The Split-off Male and Female Elements to Be Found in Men and Women', in: Ibid: *The Collected works of D.W. Winnicott* 7. 1964–1966, L. Caldwell & H. Taylor Robisnson (Eds.). Oxford University Press, 2016, pp. 317-333.
10 A. Green, 'Thirdness and Psychoanalytic Concepts', in: *The Psychoanalytic Quarterly* 73 (2004/1), pp. 99-135, p. 104.
11 S. Hartman. 'The Poetic Time Stamp of Digital Erotic Objects', in: *Psychoanalytic Perspectives* 14 (2017), pp. 159-174, p. 161.

[12] A. Jacob, 'The Demise of the Analogue Mind: Digital Primal Fantasies and the Technology of Loss-less-ness', in: S. Frosh (Ed.), *Psychosocial Imaginaries*. London: Palgrave Macmillan, 2015, pp. 126-144.

[13] By "naval logic" Amber Jacobs refers to S. Freud's first topography, which he detailed in Chapter VII of *The Interpretation of Dreams*. In this model of the mind when psychic contents are repressed, they leave a mnestic trace that can be mobilized via the preconscious and, suitably disguised, inform the dream-thought and resurface as representation in the manifest dream. If analysis can de-construct each element of the dream to be signified, there is still an essential core – Freud calls it the dream navel – that remains elusive. Jacobs emphasises that this translative model, based on dreams, implies the real presence of the object that, when lost, leaves traces and the analogic camera follows this trajectory, unlike the digital device, which creates ex novo the virtual image of an object that was never present in the first place.

[14] S. Hartman, 'Cybermourning: Grief in Flux from Object Loss to Collective Immortality', in: *Psychoanalytic Inquiry* 32 (2012), pp. 454-467, p. 460 (emphasis in the original).

[15] S. Freud, *Group Psychology*, p. 459.

[16] G. Anders, *The Obsolence of Men, vol 1*. The first volume of Anders' major work *Die Antiquiertheit des Menschen* was published in 1956, the second volume in 1980. For English translation, see: Libcom.org.

[17] Ibid., Vol. 2, see page 1: https://files.libcom.org/files/ObsolescenceofManVol%20 IIGunther%20Anders.pdf (accessed 22-20-2023).

[18] S. Freud, *Civilization and its Discontents* (1930), *SE* 21, pp. 65-146, p. 91.

[19] S. Turkle, 'Whither psychoanalysis in computer culture?', in: *Psychoanalytic Psychology* 21, pp. 16-30.

[20] E. Malater, 'Caught in the Web: Patient, Therapist, Email and the Internet' in: *Psychoanalytic Review* 94 (2007), pp. 151-168.

[21] B. Reis, 'The Analyst's Listening: For, To, With', in: *International Journal of Psychoanalysis* 102/2 (2023), pp. 219-235, p. 230.

[22] T. Ogden, *The Primitive Edge of Experience*.

[23] I. Parker, 'Psychoanalytic Cyberspace, beyond Psychology', in: *Psychoanalytic Review* 94/1 (2007), pp. 63-82, p. 74 (emphasis in the original).

[24] A. Jacobs, 'The Demise of the Analogue Mind', p. 138.

[25] S. Žižek, 'What Can Psychoanalysis Tell Us about Cyberspace?', in: *Psychoanalytic Review* 91, pp. 801-830.

[26] M. Klein, *Envy and Gratitude and Other Works 1946-64*. New York: Free Press, 1957.

[27] P.-C. Racamier, *L'incest et l'incestuel*. Paris: Dunod, 1995, p. 47 (my translation).

Ideology, Leaders, and Group Action in the January 6 Insurrection

Ricardo Ainslie

Introduction

The rise of authoritarian mindsets and group processes is in evidence throughout the world and these movements share critical features. Complex dynamics are at play within these groups, involving the character of their constituencies, the role of ideology, and their relationship to their leaders. These are factors at work in mass movements such as the Reichsbürger movement in Germany, Bolsonaro's movement in Brazil, and Donald Trump's Make America Great Again (MAGA) movement in the United States. All have succeeded in severely stressing, and at times fracturing, the institutional frameworks that structure their respective social systems. Adherents of these movements argue that the reigning government structures in their countries are illegitimate, and politicians, elections, and government entities that are obstacles to their ideological aims are targets of attack. Social media platforms including Twitter, Facebook, Truth Social, Telegram, and One American News, as well as radio and television programming such as Fox News in the United States, are the central vehicles for the dissemination of disinformation, conspiracy theories, and ideological propaganda around which their viewership becomes organized and through which this viewership finds a sense of purpose and shared identity. These ingredients form a very dangerous mix; they can be a formula for destructive social processes and the creation of mass movements which have proclivities for violence. On January 6, 2020, partisans of Donald Trump and his MAGA movement converged on Washington, D.C. for a series of rallies and protests against the American election that had been held the prior November. This gathering of Trump supporters became a violent action eventuating in a mob taking over the U.S. Capitol. They caused millions of dollars of damage, threatened the lives of American legislators, and injured over 100 police officers. Five people died.

In this chapter I draw from Sigmund Freud's ideas about group psychology as well as the work of other theorists to examine the January 6, 2020, insurrection in Washington, D.C. by Donald Trump's followers. The incident is taken as a case study of group psychology and its impact on behavior, including the relationship between partisans and their leaders. The questions to be explored include the relationship between mass movements and individual identity, the role of ideology and group leaders, as well as the impact of group psychology on human behavior. The events of January 6, 2020, in Washington, D.C., form an unusual opportunity as a psychoanalytic case study of group process and human behavior given the detailed information that is available on its origins and what took place that day.

The Group and the Individual

There are many different kinds of groups, given that groups vary in purpose, form, and size. Otto Kernberg provides an excellent framework for thinking about the relationship between group structure and the degree of regression that might be found within a group.[1] The more the life of a group is organized and bound by rules and established practices, the less the group is vulnerable to primitive regressive forces that lead to dangerous ruptures and the emergence of raw, unmetabolized primitive processes from the unconscious, including proclivities toward violence. In his classic work on the subject, *Group Psychology and Analysis of the Ego,* Freud is careful to distinguish the psychology of "mobs" or "crowds" from more institutionalized forms of groups, such as the army or religious groups.[2] The former tend to be loosely configured and are often formed around spontaneous events and circumstances. The violence that erupted in many American cities after the murder of George Floyd by Minneapolis police in 2020, when spontaneously formed groups displayed their rage by burning and looting in the streets, is one illustration. The riots in Paris and other French cities in the summer of 2023, following the police shooting of Nahel H., an unarmed 17-year-old Algerian teenager, is another among many such examples. Other forms of collective violence begin with a convening of partisans who share ideologies and grievances and which, either by design or circumstance, eventuate in violence. These groups have comparatively more structure as a function of an articulated, shared ideology. They are also given a degree of scaffolding by the political organization that has brought them together. These groups may or may not become violent, depending on circumstances such as the specific socio-historical context that has brought them together, the character of the ideology they share, and the interests of those who are in positions of leadership. It is groups such as these, the spontaneous "mobs" and thinly structured, easily incited "crowds", that Freud addresses in *Group Psychology*.

Freud is especially interested in conceptualizing the varied and peculiar ways in which "mobs" can exert themselves upon their members, changing how they act, think, and feel. He leans heavily on an earlier work by Gustave Le Bon, *Psychologie des Foules* (1895), which Freud describes as "deservedly famous" at the time, and in which Le Bon provides extensive descriptions of the psychology of the individual upon becoming part of a group, noting that the impact of the group on the individual is quite powerful

> Whoever be the individuals that compose it, however like or unlike be their mode of life, their occupations, their character, or their intelligence, the fact that they have been transformed into a group puts them in possession of a sort of collective mind which makes them feel, think, and act in a manner quite different from that in which each individual of them would feel, think, and act were he in a state of isolation.[3] There are certain ideas and feelings which do not come into being, or do not transform themselves into acts except in the case of individuals forming a group. The psychological group is a provisional being formed of heterogeneous elements, which for a moment are combined, exactly as the cells which constitute a living body form by their reunion a new being which displays characteristics very different from those possessed by each of the cells singly.[4]

Groups, in other words, have a powerfully transformative effect on those who become part of them. Le Bon is describing a particular kind of group, more in the spirit of a mob that forms in reaction to a particular circumstance or an inciting incident. Freud is in agreement with Le Bon's description of these processes, which include the loss of autonomy of thought and action and a collective regression to more "primitive" modes of being and thinking. Within the group process, individuals lose their critical faculties and are more likely to follow the dictates of the "group mind" which has erased their own perspectives and replaced them with the imperatives of the group.

Freud cites Le Bon's argument that once a person becomes caught up within the group process, there are ideas, feelings, and acts that emerge that are specific to the group and that would not otherwise exist for that person. The group transforms the individual who, in turn, behaves atypically as a function of this altered state. Thus, the group exerts enormous power over the individual, whose identity is effaced as they are folded into the "collective mind". Freud sees in this line of description an argument for psychoanalytic conceptions of the superego. The superego is sufficiently weakened by the group process that repressed and unconscious modes of being are allowed to emerge. It is this subversion of the superego that Freud views as the source of disinhibition and loss of control that is fostered by the group process. Freud also cites Le Bon's argument that the relative anonymity of the individual within the group context furthers disinhibition. In other words, once within a group, people often have a proclivity to behave in ways that are at odds with their ordinary functioning.

Le Bon denotes three factors as being at work in this kind of group process. First, the fact that one is within a group (and here, the sheer number of people who are part of the group can be a variable), often produces a sense of "'invincible power'" which permits the individual to "yield to instincts which, had he been alone, he would perforce have been kept under restraint."[5] The relative anonymity provided by the group removes a sense of responsibility for personal action. Secondly, Le Bon suggests that contagion is a powerful force within groups, leading individuals to sacrifice personal for collective interests. Finally, the group also heightens suggestibility among its members, which Le Bon likens to the experience of hypnotic suggestion which may be even more intensively at work given the power of the group process.

Ideology and Group Process

In *Group Psychology* Freud also deploys William McDougall's (*The Group Mind*, 1920) observations to shed light on a dimension of groups that Le Bon fails to address, namely the role of ideology or group belief in organizing and keeping a group together. A group cannot be constituted, psychologically speaking, unless its members have something in common with one another, "a common interest" or "mental homogeneity" which form the group mind.[6] No doubt, there are many variations of shared ideas that may provide the psychological and conceptual material from which a group is formed and by which it is held together, such as political ideology, shared tribulation, or shared aspiration. However, of particular interest in the current context is the role of shared ideology in the formation and maintenance of the group. Ideology can be a powerful organizer of groups, and Freud cites McDougall's argument that groups amplify their members' emotional engagement with shared belief systems and ideological commitments, what he calls the "exaltation or intensification of emotion" that is a product of the group.[7] McDougall argued that the greater the size of the group, the greater the intensity of this shared feeling or the more powerful the emotional amplification of the felt connection to the ideological commitment.

The Group's Relationship to the Leader

Throughout *Group Psychology* Freud draws extensively and, for the most part, approvingly, from the ideas of Le Bon and McDougall. However, in Freud's view, Le Bon does not succeed in bringing the function of the leader into adequate alignment with Le Bon's observations about how groups behave. It is here, in the realm of the role of the leader, that Freud stakes out a distinctly psychoanalytic position. When Le Bon toys with the notion of the "herd instinct", Freud views this as quite limited in explaining the leader's role within the group.

> What Le Bon says on the subject of leaders of groups is less exhaustive and does not enable us to make out an underlying principle so clearly. He thinks that as soon as living beings are gathered together in certain numbers, no matter whether they are a herd of animals or a collection of human beings, they place themselves instinctively under the authority of a chief.[8]

Freud acknowledges the group's desire or need for a leader but asserts that the leader's characteristics are important in defining the extent to which they can play that role.

> Although in this way the needs of a group carry it half-way to meet the leader, yet he too must fit in with it in his personal qualities. He must himself be held in fascination by a strong faith (in an idea) in order to awaken the group's faith; he must possess a strong and imposing will, which the group, which has no will of its own, can accept from him.[9]

Freud argues that identification, the earliest form of object tie in which the ego assumes the characteristics of the object, is a core process at work in relation between group members and the group's leader. Of particular interest is Freud's argument that the identificatory process in relation to the leader has powerful implications for the relationship of group members to one another. The mutual tie between the members of the group centers on their shared identification with the leader, which creates powerful emotional ties between the group members themselves. As Freud notes, "A primary group of this kind is a number of individuals who have put one and the same object in the place of their ego ideal and have consequently identified themselves with one another in their ego."[10] Like Le Bon, Freud views suggestion as playing an important part in groups, although his position is more complex given that Freud argues that suggestion is coming *both* from the leader as well as from "every individual upon every other individual" in the group.[11]

More recently, Volkan[12] and Kernberg[13] have theorized about the role of idealized, narcissistic leaders in the mobilization of regressive processes in large groups. Volkan's contribution centers on his understanding of how broader social and cultural contexts contribute to regression in large groups. As a country, the United States has undergone significant social transformation in recent decades. The country experienced two catastrophic economic downturns, as well as the Coronavirus epidemic, for example, in addition to profound demographic changes spurred in part by immigration that have created tremendous anxieties in some quarters, anxieties that Donald Trump made his primary talking points. These conditions set the stage for group regression and create fertile ground for leaders to shape group process as they articulate shared ideologies around which collective identities coalesce.[14] Malignant, narcissistic leaders can exert tremendous destructive power over a group under these conditions.[15] They offer an idealized object with whom the group can identify, and who provides promise and hope that their concerns and anxieties will be addressed. In this way, the group feels affirmed and protected, but also feels a profound connection to the leader who has great power over the group by virtue of group's tremendous needs and the identifications that cement the tie between the group and the leader.[16]

The January 6th 2020: A Case Study of Group Process and Political Action

Donald Trump's MAGA movement represents a broad and multifaceted collection of interests and political aims. It has also grown from a seemingly farfetched political ambition in 2015 to a massive political movement (in the 2019 presidential election in the United States Trump garnered over 70 million votes and his popularity, notwithstanding two impeachments and multiple criminal charges, remained steadfast among members of his Republican party). The object of our current interest is the gathering of Trump supporters in Washington, D.C. on the January 6, 2020. While it had been a hallmark of Trump's politics to hold large rallies around the country, this gathering was different. It was much larger than Trump's prior rallies given that multiple Trump-supporting organizations were involved in turning out their members via a coordinated campaign. It was also different in that it eventuated in an unprecedented violent attack on the American Capitol building while the congress was in session for the purpose of certifying the American presidential election which had been held the previous November 6, 2019.

A short American civics lesson is required to understand the context for the January 6 insurrection. In the American system, each state is granted a number of electoral votes (together called the Electoral College) which are in play only during presidential elections. These are assigned to each state in proportion to their population. In American presidential elections, the candidate with the greatest number of total electoral votes is declared the winner of the contest. This system purports to balance out the interests (and political representation) of those living in sparsely populated states (say, Montana or South Dakota) as opposed to those living in denser states (say, New York or Texas). The system is rather cumbersome, and, at times awkward for the American democracy, for an American presidential candidate can under some circumstances win more Electoral College votes than their opponent (by winning a higher percentage of the sparsely populated states) while actually losing the "popular" vote. This occurred, in fact, during the 2016 presidential election in which Donald Trump won the majority of the Electoral College votes while losing the popular vote by over three-million votes.

The Electoral College votes from each state are certified by the U.S. Congress in January following presidential elections (which take place in November every four years). By that time, votes have been cast and counted and the electoral votes for each state in which a candidate won the popular vote have been allotted to them. On January 6, 2020, the Vice-President of the United States was to preside over the official presentation of the Electoral College votes and thereby certify the results of the November election in which Joseph Biden had defeated Donald Trump (Biden had won both the popular vote and the Electoral College vote). The convening of the American Congress to ratify the Electoral College votes is merely ceremonial. Or so it had been until January 6, 2020, when Donald Trump supporters came to Washington, D.C. with the intent of protesting the election which, since the November election loss, Trump had falsely asserted was fraudulent and stolen.

Even prior to the November 6, 2019, election, Donald Trump had been asserting at rallies and in other speeches (as well as in a frenetic flow of tweets), with no evidence, that the election was threatened by an effort by his opponents to steal the election from him and his supporters. He repeatedly warned his followers that the future of America itself was at stake, and in this way, on a national level, stirred his followers to believe extensive efforts to deceive them were afoot. Thus, he was successful at establishing a certain restive and emotionally heightened climate among many of his followers. In the immediate aftermath of the November 6 election, Trump and his inner circle refused to accept the results. There followed a cascade of accusations and assertions with myriad plots to suggest that the election had indeed been stolen and illegitimate. Of 62 court challenges brought in state and Federal courts, including the United States Supreme Court, during this time, Trump lost all except for one inconsequential case.[17] In several states, votes were recounted (in one state three times). Many of the court challenges were before judges that Trump himself had appointed, and all of the vote recounts produced essentially the same results. Trump's Attorney General would soon state that after review, there was no evidence of widespread fraud or of fraud of a nature that would have changed the election results in any state,[18] yet the Trump partisans refused to accept the results of the election.

It was in the context of this tumultuous post-election, that Trump called upon his followers to converge on Washington, D.C. on January 6th, 2020, in order to "Stop the Steal" as he put it. Trump promised that it would be "wild." Thousands of Trump supporters, from ordinary Republican voters to members of pro-Trump militia groups, heeded his call. On January 6th, 2020, some 30,000-50,000 Trump supporters descended upon Washington eager to support him. The exact figures are unknown; there were three separate rallies in various Washington locations culminating in Trump's speech at the Ellipse, according to the Congressional Select Committee's final report. However, 28,000 attended Trump's speech at the Ellipse.[19] While many came prepared for some sort of violence (the Secret Service confiscated 269 knives or blades, 242 cannisters of pepper spray, 18 brass knuckles, 18 tasers, and 30 "batons or blunt instruments" as rally-goers passed through the magnetometers[20], it is likely that most of those who came had unclear notions of what lay ahead. The violent assault on the Capitol was not a premeditated action on their part; "Stop the Steal" was but a vague, ill-defined rallying cry with no specific roadmap for how they might alter the election results. They came for the camaraderie, for the carnivalesque character of the moment, and they came to protest what they believed to be an injustice, as countless of American protesters had done in the past with respect to many different causes. On January 6, many of Trump's inner circle gave speeches to the gathered crowd repeating the narratives of a stolen election and encouraging action to stop the certification of the Electoral College votes. The speeches culminated with Donald Trump reiterating these points and directing the attendees to go to the Capitol, where he would "be there" to join them.

Three Distinct Groups

One limitation of the inferences about group process found in *Group Psychology and Analysis of the Ego* is the assumption that groups become somewhat homogenous once their dynamics are activated. With respect to the events that were unleashed on January 6, three distinct subgroups are discernible amongst the participants. All were Trump supporters who, to various degrees, subscribed to the Trumpian worldview including the belief that the American election had been marked by irregularities and fraud and that the election had been stolen from Donald Trump. However, not all of those who came to Washington, D.C. participated in the direct actions on the Capitol. Roughly 30,000 – 50,000 Trump supporters came to Washington, D.C. for the January 6 protests and slightly more than half of these attended Trump's speech on the Ellipse.[21] Of these, approximately 10,000 marched on to the Capitol. Thus, a significant portion of those who attended the Trump speech (and other speeches) that day did not respond to Trump's call and did not move on to participate in the assault on the Capitol. This fact is somewhat at odds with the assertions made in *Group Psychology.* How to account for those who were motivated to come to Washington, D.C. to support Trump, who attended the speeches aimed at "inflaming their passions," and who heard Trump's call to march to the Capitol but declined the invitation?

Of those who heeded Trump's call, there were two distinct subgroups. The first, the largest in their number, were sufficiently engaged and aroused by the speeches, and sufficiently moved by a cumulative sense that they and Trump had been wronged, that they wished to take their protest to the Capitol itself. However, it is difficult to know for sure what, specifically, was their intent. As the prosecutions of those who participated in the attack have shown, while some had come armed with makeshift weapons (poles, bear spray, etc.), most had not. It is this group that most conforms to the "mob" or "crowd" which is the subject of *Group Psychology.* They fell into a psychological space where

147

the variables of anonymity (or relative anonymity – some traveled with friends and even with family members), suggestion, and contagion, as well as the influence of a powerful leader, all conspired to create a group process that eventuated in the breach of police lines, entry into the Capitol, and, for some, participation in the pursuit of Congressmen and Senators identified through their favored social media and news outlets as "the enemy." They were swept up in the charged emotional atmosphere of the moment, and it is likely that they fell under the "hypnotic" sway of their leader whom they idealized and with whom they identified, while also being powerfully influenced by the crowd itself, that is, by the processes of contagion and suggestion. The power of the group dynamic erased their individual autonomy as they became part of Le Bon's "group mind."

The regressive processes described by Freud and Le Bon are clearly in evidence in this group, including the radical disinhibitions, such as attacking police lines, and destroying property once inside the Capitol. Individuals who have been prosecuted and convicted make it evident that most of these Trump supporters were "ordinary citizens" (farmers, attorneys, shop keepers, police, current or former military, teachers, etc.) and Trump adherents of long standing but without prior histories of violent behavior. To an astounding degree, the descriptions of group behavior that one finds in *Group Psychology* are precisely what we find in these participants' actions that day.

The militia groups (primarily the Oath Keepers, Proud Boys, and 3-Percenters) form the second of the two discernible subgroups that attacked the Capitol that day. Three to four hundred of them came prepared for the actions that took place.[22] They were organized and disciplined militias who brought plans, body armor, communications equipment, and a variety of weapons. On the ground, they acted as inciters and directors. They reconnoitered the Capitol for its vulnerabilities and gave directions to the crowd while directly encouraging them to seize the Capitol.[23] Several members of these groups have been tried and convicted of seditious conspiracy – that is, for being part of a coordinated effort to interfere with the American government. These groups conform more with the "organized" or "artificial" groups described by Freud in *Group Psychology,* groups like the army or the church. Unlike the group described above, the militia groups were not "swept away" and did not fall under the influence of the group. Their actions were methodical, preconceived, and had a certain coherence as opposed to the acts of a mob under the sway of a powerful leader and the regressive force of the group process. They were accelerants of the more regressive processes that took hold of the first, and by far larger, group that moved on the Capitol that day.

Thus, there were three distinct clusters of Trump supporters present on January 6. Those partisans who were there for the speeches but chose not to move on the Capitol, and the two groups that did assault the Capitol. Of the latter, the largest consisted of the unorganized supporters, the "mob," while the second consisted of the various militias. The Proud Boys even referred to the first group that took part in the assault as the "normies" – that is, ordinary people who had come to Washington, D.C. driven by their beliefs and convictions but who were not part of the hardcore "Stop the Steal" militia contingent intent on violent action.[24] The militias played an important role in laying the groundwork for what was to come, which included inciting the "normies" into action when the time came to activate that next step in their strategy.

Ideology, Identity, and Political Action

The January 6 participants who were part of the attack on the Capitol conform to Freud's and McDougall's views in *Group Psychology* regarding the role of ideology. They were "held together" by a shared "idea" – an ideological structure which motivated them to come to Washington, D.C. in the first place. Once there, they were swept up in the dynamics of the group, both by processes of identification with Trump as leader as well as the "contagion" created by the mutual inter-identifications amongst the participants themselves.

In *Group Psychology* Freud discusses identification (with a leader, with other members of the group), and, as noted, he addresses the notion that ideology, as a shared belief, can be a kind of psychological glue that binds a group together. While Le Bon and McDougall both implicate the role of ideology in the dynamics of group process, and Le Bon specifically suggests that it is shared faith "in an idea" that links the crowd to the leader, McDougall underscores that for people to constitute a group in a psychological sense they must "have something in common with one another, a common interest in an object, a similar emotional bias in some situation or other and [...] 'some degree of reciprocal influence'".[25] However, Freud does not explore the relationship between ideology and identity, per se. This is due to the fact that the construct of identity, as we deploy it today, did not come into play in the psychoanalytic literature until the publication of Erik Erikson's classic, *Childhood & Society* (1950). It is here that the work of Vamik Volkan[26] is useful in helping us more fully understand identity processes in the context of large groups.

Volkan focuses on the developmental origins of large group identities in which we participate, and which organize us. These include racial and ethnic, religious, class, gender, and other kinds of large-group identities in relation to which our individual identities are shaped. In addition to the familial variables from which personal identity is fashioned, over the course of development we also come to understand the role of what Volkan terms "large canvas" dimensions within which we are implicated.[27] For example, in early elementary school years children begin to grasp the concepts of race and ethnicity, they may come to understand their religious affiliation as distinct from the religious affiliations that other children have, they may begin to discern social status distinctions within the culture they inhabit, etc. By adolescence, according to Volkan, these larger social and cultural positionalities have been internalized and have become woven into individual identity.[28] Volkan likens these variables to a kind of outer garment that may remain a backdrop, or implicit, until such times as political currents, for example, or some other social stressor (ethnic conflict, a traumatizing incident, etc.) bring them into relief, mobilizing those who share this "outer garment." For Americans, the terrorist acts associated with September 11, 2001, are an illustration. In the aftermath, Americans came together in ways that seemed unprecedented (unless one was alive, say, when Japan launched a surprise attack in Hawaii that sunk most of the American Pacific fleet in Pearl Harbor). The murder of George Floyd in Minneapolis, is another such example. It galvanized the African American community in the United States, bringing forth tens of thousands of Black people (and eventually their allies as well). In France in the summer of 2023, the police shooting of a 17 year-old Algerian youth is yet another illustration. The "shared garment" of racial and ethnic identity was activated in these incidents. In the case of George Floyd, it resulted in the national Black Lives Matter movement. The point is that specific events can trigger collective identities that have been implicit or part of what is felt and known but only episodically reflected upon.

Volkan's ideas help us conceptualize the January 6 Capitol action as one in which political ideology is a "shared garment" connecting those who came to Washington, D.C. to participate in the protests. They had been mobilized by a specific, *perceived* trauma – the false belief that their leader, Donald Trump, had been a victim of electoral fraud and that the election had been stolen from them. This shared political identity had been formed over the course of several years, shaped by a constant flow of ideologically charged notions which unified a disparate group of individuals into a community that shared an interpretation of contemporary American social and political life.

Myriad conspiracy theories continuously washed over them via favored news outlets and social media, reinforcing these ideological identities. The group psychology at work post-election and on January 6 drew from this "shared garment." The tens of thousands of MAGA partisans who came to Washington, D.C. were already part of a clear, identifiable group, linked together by a mix of political ideology and belief in a charismatic leader to whom they felt deeply connected. It is this very context that lends itself to the forces of "suggestion" and "contagion" theorized by Le Bon and by Freud, and to the regressive group processes described by Kernberg and Volkan. People who are deeply immersed in political projects have deep attachments to these ideas – anything that challenges them or that becomes an obstacle to their realization becomes a target of attack because a threat to the ideology represents a threat to the self. They are also hyper defended against information that is at odds with their ideological constructions. In this instance, losing scores of legal challenges and recounts that only confirmed the fact that their candidate had lost did nothing to alter their shared conviction that Trump (and themselves) were victims of corruption and fraud.

Conclusion

In *Group Psychology* Freud provides a rich description of group behavior and the forces that drive people to act as they do in group contexts. These insights are as pertinent today as they were a century ago. The regression at work in groups has various sources including the effects of relative anonymity within the group and the forces of contagion with respect to the group itself and suggestion, especially in relation to the leader. These exert a powerful effect on the individual within a group. Freud remarks on the impact of the group process on the superego, leading to disinhibition and the activation of more primitive psychological processes from within the unconscious. In addition, Freud underscores the factors at work in the group member's identification with the leader through which the leader is internalized, and, how the identifications with the leader create shared identifications among the group participants. In fact, Freud was of the view that perhaps theorists tend to over emphasize the role of the leader while not paying sufficient attention to the shared identifications and the mutual influence of group members upon one another.

The importance of "shared ideas" or ideology in the formation of the group and as the "glue" that maintains the group is noted in *Group Psychology*,

Ricardo Ainslie

although it is fair to say that Freud does not explore the importance of ideology in shaping the group. This is largely due to the fact that the kinds of groups that Freud had in mind were spontaneously formed "mobs" or "crowds," where ideological frameworks may not be as important. The January 6 insurrectionists, on the other hand, while displaying many of the behaviors and dynamics addressed by Freud, illustrate the power of ideology as an organizing force. The powerful identifications at work in relation to their leader, Donald Trump, together with their deep connection to Trumpian ideology and belief system, played the critical role in mobilizing the tens of thousands of January 6 protesters.

Group Psychology tends to assume that groups have a somewhat monolithic character. The January 6 protesters reflect a more complex and multi-faceted character. As I have sought to illustrate, they actually comprised three different kinds of groups: Those who came to protest and who participated in the carnivalesque aspects of the event and listened to the speeches by Trump and his inner circle but did not march on the Capitol. The second kind of group were what the Proud Boys called "normies." The "normies" had come to protest and were deeply committed to the MAGA cause and to Trump as their leader, but it appears that most did not come with a premeditated goal of violently attacking the Capitol and hunting down politicians who they viewed as "enemies." The "normies" best fit the behavior of individuals caught up in a group process as described by Freud in *Group Psychology*. Finally, the militia groups had a different profile. They were not "swept away" by the regressive power of the group process. Rather, they had some of the characteristics of Freud's "artificial" groups, such as the army and the church – they had articulated plans and were trained, disciplined, and came prepared for violent action. All three groups were strongly identified with the political ideology of the MAGA movement and strongly identified with Trump as their leader.

Perhaps the MAGA members who came to Washington, D.C. but did not participate in the storming of the Capitol are the most interesting. In *Group Psychology* Freud hypothesizes that people intersect with group processes in idiosyncratic ways, which have to do with the particulars of their development within a familial context. These differences may account for those who did not participate in the actual assault on the Capitol. Other variables may explain this group as well, such as varying degrees of identification with Trump as a leader, including variations in the extent to which they subscribed to MAGA ideology – they subscribed enough to come to Washington, D.C., but not enough to march onto the Capitol.

The MAGA movement, more broadly, is a testament to the power of ideology to influence and shape thought and perception. Many of the January 6 partisans held tightly to their beliefs, notwithstanding factual evidence to the contrary. Many appear to have lost the capacity to critique and objectively assess. Years after the fact, notwithstanding media coverage, Congressional hearings, or the thousands of hours of video, many adherents remain fixed in their ideological positions and their interpretation of what took place that day, including many who deny that the attack was violent or who deny that the actors were MAGA partisans.

As a leader, Trump played an instrumental role both as an idealized object of identification and as a shaper of the ideological frame that connected the insurrectionists to one another and to him. Kernberg[29] is especially helpful in illustrating how a leader's pathological narcissism, with the accompanying interest in bending the group's interests to the leader's will, can lead to highly destructive consequences, which is what happened on January 6.

Perhaps the greatest challenge to civic life is how to intervene when historical circumstances create a dangerous mix of disaffected citizens, a powerful narcissistic leader who articulates and manipulates their grievances, and toxic ideology which holds them all together. These are the conditions that engender mass violence.

Notes

[1] Cf. O. Kernberg, *Ideology, Conflict, and Leadership in Groups and Organizations.* New Haven: Yale Univ. Press, 1998 and O. Kernberg, 'Malignant Narcissism and Large Group Regression,' in: *The Psychoanalytic Quarterly* 89/1 (2020), pp. 1-24.

[2] S. Freud, *Group Psychology and the Analysis of the Ego* (1921), *SE* 18, pp. 65-144, p. 93 ff.

[3] Note, Freud is clear regarding his disagreement with Le Bon as to the ultimate origins of these behaviors. Freud is not of the view that within the group new characteristics and behaviors are brought forth. Instead, Freud argues that what is tapped by the group process are primaeval elements that form the core of who we are, a core typically well concealed (more or less) by the superego and defensive operations that keep these deep in the unconscious. What we see emerging within the group are the latent propensities that live within every person, a notion that is tightly woven into the Freudian view of human nature.

[4] Ibid., p. 73.

[5] Ibid., p. 74.

[6] Ibid., p. 83.

7 Ibid., p. 84.
8 Ibid., p. 80 f.
9 Ibid., p. 81.
10 Ibid., p. 116 (emphasis in the original).
11 Ibid., p. 118.
12 Cf. V. D. Volkan, *The Need to Have Enemies and Allies: From Clinical Practice to International Relationships*. Northvale, NJ: Jason Aronson, 1988 and V. D. Volkan, *Bloodlines: From Ethnic Pride to Ethnic Terrorism*, New York: Farrar, Straus and Giroux, 1997.
13 Cf. O. Kernberg, *Ideology, Conflict, and Leadership in Groups and Organizations*, New Haven: Yale Univ. Press, 1998 and O. Kernberg: 'Malignant Narcissism and Large Group Regression'.
14 Cf. V. D. Volkan: *Blind Trust*, Charlottesville, VA: Pitchstone Publishing, 2004.
15 Cf. O. Kernberg, 'Malignant Narcissism and Large Group Regression'.
16 Ibid.
17 *Final Report: Select Committee to Investigate the January 6th Attack on the United States Capitol*. December 22, 2022, 117th Congress Second Session, House Report 117-663.
18 Ibid., p. 373.
19 Ibid., p. 640.
20 Ibid., p. 640.
21 Ibid., p. 640.
22 Ibid., p. 642.
23 Ibid., p. 640.
24 N. Reneau, S. Cooper, A. Feuer & A. Byrd, 'How the Proud Boys Breached the Capitol on Jan 6.', in: *The New York Times* June 17, 2022. https://www.nytimes.com/video/us/politics/100000008392796/rile-up-the-normies-how-proud-boys-breached-the-capitol.html (accessed 18-06-2023).
25 S. Freud, *Group Psychology*, p. 84.
26 V. D. Volkan, *The Need to Have Enemies and Allies*, and V. D. Volkan, *Bloodlines: From Ethnic Pride to Ethnic Terrorism*, New York: Farrar, Straus and Giroux, 1997.
27 V. D. Volkan, *Bloodlines*.
28 V. D. Volkan, *The Need to Have Enemies and Allies*, and V. D. Volkan. *Bloodlines*.
29 O. Kernberg, 'Malignant Narcissism and Large Group Regression', in: *The Psychoanalytic Quarterly* 89/1 (2020), p. 1-24.

Massenpsychologie and MAGA

Gail Newman

One hundred years after the publication of Sigmund Freud's essay *Massenpsychologie und Ich-Analyse* (1921) a striking scene played itself out at the United States Capitol: more than two thousand people stormed the building in search of Congressmembers to intimidate into preventing the certification of Joseph Biden's election, in November 2020, to the office of President of the United States. Refusing to accept the defeat of their candidate, Donald Trump, the marchers constituted a mob if ever there was one; it was large, unruly, and simmering with resentment that threatened to bubble over into violence at any time. Indeed, five people died in the direct context of the riot and many were injured; the insurrection caused $1.5 million in damage to the Capitol. It is tempting to regard the January 6 marchers as reproducing the conditions of the mass as defined by Freud: "a number of individuals who have put one and the same object in the place of their ego ideal and have consequently identified themselves with one another in their ego."[1] After all, the group was centered on – and instigated by, according to the House of Representatives investigation into the incident – a single idealized individual, and the individuals in the group were so closely identified with one another via the vague yet grandiose goal of "making America great again" that any differences among them seemed to disappear.

Indeed, in important ways the MAGA movement aligns with Freud's 1921 model, especially in its affective intensity and the blindness of its devotion to its central figure. But a closer look reveals profound changes in the conditions that Freud took for granted when penning his essay. Specifically, what structurally oriented psychoanalysts have termed the *Third* – the principle, linked but not identical to the paternal function, that authorizes a shared sense of moral and epistemological reality – has been eroded in the context of neoliberal thinking to the point of nearly disappearing. Further, in presupposing an unquestioned paternal function that drives the psychology of the group, Freud's essay occludes the role of maternal functioning in group dynamics. I contend that today's right-wing mass groups both reflect and enact the utter lack of a meaning-making Third and the terrifying absence of care that characterize contemporary Western societies.

Freud promises that his essay will get to the bottom of the phenomena outlined by Gustave Le Bon in his *Psychologie des foules*, which focuses on the quasi-hypnotic effect of the mass on its individual members. Under this effect, whatever agency and conscience individuals had possessed is eclipsed by the sense of omnipotence – but also vulnerability – instilled in them by the mass. The work of other thinkers, notably Williams McDougall's *The Group* Mind (1920) is also included in Freud's summary of the previous findings on mass psychology:

> We started from the fundamental fact that an individual in a group is subjected through its influence to what is often a profound alteration in his mental activity. His liability to affect becomes extraordinarily intensified, while his intellectual ability is markedly reduced.[2]

While Freud acknowledges the thoroughness and accuracy of previous thinkers' detailing of the *effects* of the mass, he is convinced that a "logical foundation"[3] of these effects is lacking. He finds such an explanation in the exigencies of the libido, and specifically its relation to the father, which he illustrates with the examples of two "extremely lasting ones" and "highly organized" groups, the (Catholic) church and the army. Each group relies on a twofold libidinal bond for the maintenance of its integrity: individual members bond simultaneously with the other members of the group and with the group's "father" figure, who in the case of the church is Christ and in the army the general.[4] In both instances, the coherence of the group is conditioned by the assumption that the "father" loves each of his "children" equally:

> This equal love was expressly enunciated by Christ: 'Inasmuch as ye have done it unto one of the least of these my brethren, ye have done it unto me.' [...] The like holds good of an army. The Commander-in-Chief is a father who loves all soldiers equally, and for that reason they are comrades among themselves.[5]

In the absence of these conditions, the groups would collapse.

Freud's exemplary groups center on an individual father figure, yes, but standing behind the particular figure is a principle upon which the entire edifice is based: reliability, universality and equity. In this respect, Freud is the heir of Immanuel Kant, whose transcendental idealism is an affirmation of abstraction: each individual's knowledge of and operation in the world is based on an unchanging and impersonal set of moral and epistemological laws and functions. These self-evident principles constitute what contemporary psychoanalysts call Thirdness. In his essay 'Why the Pair Needs the Third', John Muller delineates, based on work by Samuel Gerson, three kinds of Third: developmental, relational, and, most relevant to mass psychology, the structural Third, which must be in place in order for a "shared authority in creating and interpreting a common representational history"[6] to be able to come about. The "common representational history" – the master narratives of a society – operates in the background and frames political engagement. In the case of Freud's essay, his choice to enter into the explanation of mass psychology through discussion of valued *institutions* brings the assumption of a structural Third into view.

By Freud's own description, the structure of equal paternal love that underlies the church and the military is an "illusion," but this does not constitute grounds for illegitimacy. On the contrary, this illusion is aligned with what Muller calls "the only usable third", namely "one that is *already shared before it is experienced as shared*"[7]. In Lacanian terms, this is the "Other with a capital O, [...] the very foundation of intersubjectivity"[8]; it is the "guarantor of Good Faith" and "Truth's witness".[9] It is no accident that Lacan associates this function with the *nom de père*, the Name of the Father, since it has its foundation in the Oedipus complex, which renders triangular that which had been binary. If what was at stake in the dyadic relationship between the child and its caregiver was separation and connection – and at the most primal level *existence* – at issue in the oedipal configuration is position in a social surround and attendant concerns with social status and social legitimacy. In the institutions that occupy Freud, such legitimacy is a given. As in the case of individual psychology, oedipal triangularity in the group means that its libidinal energy is paradoxically both generated and contained by the assumption of equal access of all members – by default male – to paternal recognition.[10] Indeed, the perpetuation of the oedipal cycle propels our patriarchal society: what the younger generation of men loses in the struggle with the older generation over paternal possessions (the woman, the territory, the company) is ultimately more than compensated by the legitimacy gained through ascending to the paternal position in the next generation.

As Muller notes, "[...] the structural Third is not a determinate subject or object but rather a logical structure, structuring our thinking and our relationship to each other and to the world"[11]. Freud's paradigmatic groups demonstrate how this operates, in characteristic form by way of the negative.

The largest portion of Freud's discussion is devoted to an examination of the origin of the *panic* that leads to the dissolution of the libidinal bonds holding the groups together. Starting with the army, Freud disagrees with McDougall and others who regard the magnitude of danger as decisive for the emergence of group-threatening panic. Instead, he reads backwards from the disintegration of bonding to a more fundamental breakdown: "The fact is, therefore, that panic fear *presupposes* a relaxation in the libidinal structure of the group [...]."[12] What has set the stage for panic, according to Freud is "[t]he loss of the leader in some sense or other, the birth of misgivings about him"[13] ("Irrewerden an ihm"). The notion of "Irrewerden" is key here: Freud is not talking so much about the loss of the particular father figure – the death of a commander, for example – as about the loss of faith in the paternal function. That is, the reliable existence of Thirdness has been brought into question.

This is precisely the state in which we find ourselves today, due, I maintain, to the rise of neoliberalism. Over the last approximately 40 years, the market has slid into the place of the Third that "structures our thinking and our relationship to each other and the world"[14]. At base, the theory behind neoliberalism derives directly from Enlightenment thinking insofar as it taps into the idea of a transcendent, objective realm, but in a distorted fashion. Its founder was Friedrich August von Hayek, an Austrian-British economist whose work, virtually ignored at the time of its publication in the early twentieth century, was revived in the 1980s by Margaret Thatcher, Ronald Reagan, and their followers. According to its proponents, the market is a purely abstract – and hence morally and politically neutral – structure that governs all aspects of human interaction. The market is said to exist beyond all individual political, cultural, or personal agendas; it is supposedly governed by a price structure that is akin to mathematics in the givenness of its validity. At least since the 1980s, we have been taught to embrace wholeheartedly the idea that human beings are at base *homo economicus*, a species guided by the perfectly rational laws of the market, where self-interest is defined entirely in terms of maximizing personal gain and relationships are entirely transactional.[15]

This philosophy drives and ostensibly justifies the extreme wealth inequality between the Global North and the Global South and, in microcosm, within the United States. The notion that there is such a thing as a societal whole to which each individual belongs, for which each individual is responsible, and from which each individual can gain benefit has progressively disappeared, and with it an authentic structuring Third. In its place are the dictates of the market, which represent a kind of pseudo-Third. It operates in the background like the Third, determining our thinking and behavior to a large extent invisibly and unconsciously. But its fundamental orientation is not triangular but binary. Zero-sum thinking prevails in a neoliberal context: if you gain, I lose. Far from "creat[ing] boundaries [and] consensual laws" that can bring about "the possibility for genuine remembering and mourning, and for acts of agency and acts of meaning"[16], market thinking tells us that anything goes, as long as it leads to profit and "success." In such a context, there must necessarily be winners and losers. And unlike in the originary triangular structure of the Oedipus complex, where the son understood that his "losing" of the battle for the father's possession – his renunciation of his desire for the mother – would be recouped by his eventual achievement of the coveted paternal position himself, "when Oedipus goes missing, desire can never be present to itself as anything more than remorse".[17] *Agency* devolves into sheer power, *mourning* is replaced by "allegiance to a trapped and victimized sense of self"[18], and *meaning* becomes ad hoc.

There are many losers in the neoliberal game, but those on which I am focused here are people who have imagined themselves to be in the winning position for a very long time: the white men, mostly but not exclusively working class, who could in fact for many decades reliably breathe the air of patriarchal privilege without thinking much about it, albeit in the context of deferral that attends the Oedipal structure. While the marginalized subject (e.g., the colonized, the enslaved) has always been and continues to be required to renounce without payoff, the white working-class male is now told that the expected payoff for his renunciation (working hard, saving money) is no longer available.[19] The response is a kind of supernova of white patriarchy. In Gentile's description, we are dealing with "a relative sense of impotence which can be camouflaged by a subjective omnipotence"[20] – a compensatory sense of omnipotence bolstered by the illusion of connection to a powerful father.   In the face of what they imagine is the unfair discontinuation of their transgenerational embeddedness in the paternal order, these figures search in desperation for an ersatz father who can re-integrate them into it. But this is not the father as representative of the Third. Rather, what is sought is a kind of absolute power that is aligned more closely with the all-or-nothing dyad than the productive, ongoing mediation derived from thirdness. This is not the *nom de père* but the *imago* found in the mirror; the Lacanian ego is precipitated out of this image immediately in both senses of the word: the identification is both *sudden* and *total*. But however perfect this self-aligned image might seem to be, it is irreducibly "fictional," and can be approached only "asymptotically"[21]. I was reminded of this perfectly powerful – and utterly unreal – imaginary self+prosthetic when I read the following quote from Rev. Ken Peters, pastor of the Patriot Church in Lenoir City, Tennessee: "You know [Biden's] not the most popular president in America. How many Biden parades did you see?"[22] For this MAGA-ite, a president's power is measured only in terms of his specular presence.

In this context, truth, too, is apprehended immediately, via its alignment with personal experience and with the chosen leader figure who "embodies perfect credibility" for his followers. From one perspective, truth disappears, because "the mass is absolutely certain of what it does or is willing to do. It neither aims at truth nor appears to be concerned with it". From another perspective, truth becomes absolute; the mass is "an incarnation or a supreme realization of the truth"[23]. We are dealing here with what Alan Bass calls "concreteness", the conviction that seeing is believing, and "undoubted perceptions" allow one to "conflate fantasy and reality".[24] It is a profoundly binaristic structure: my perception = the truth, my fantasy = reality, and the world = the intentions of a conspiratorial bad actor. When we dwell in Thirdness, by contrast, I recognize that my perception is a single perception living in a world of other perceptions that in turn are mediated via relationship to each other and to what Muller calls a "primary sign"[25]. This sign is, to be clear, not an Archimedean point, a site of absolute objectivity; it does not "equate to the object" of truth. Instead, it only "represents it, thereby generating the partial, probabilistic, and indefinite nature of human knowing"[26]. *Imperfection* and *process* are the hallmarks of three-dimensional truth.

The debate around Covid-19 can serve as an example of the distinction between the binaristic, concrete notion of truth and an idea of truth associated with Thirdness. The latter is enacted in the scientific method, which begins with the establishment of a hypothesis based in empirical observation or logical supposition. The hypothesis is by its very nature imperfect and demands testing, a process that takes place again and again, by various actors and through various means, resulting in a conclusion that is acknowledged by all of its authors to be preliminary. Hence when Dr. Anthony Fauci, the chief medical advisor to the American president during the Covid-19 crisis, declared in the spring of 2020 that only those with the illness or caring for someone with it needed to wear a mask and then later announced that general masking would help prevent the spread of the coronavirus, he was following the "evolving situation" of the pandemic. Fauci explained that initially, "we were not aware that 40 to 45% of people were asymptomatic, nor were we aware that a substantial proportion of people who get infected get infected from people who are without symptoms." He called the developing situation a "classic example of how guidance can change as additional scientific evidence emerges"[27]. Compare this approach to the Covid-deniers and vaccine-refusers who claimed that the shift in advice signaled *lying* by Fauci, who went on to become for them the face of evil and absolute untruth who paired perfectly with their icon of absolute truth, his boss Donald Trump.

Freud's discussion of identification in the *Massenpsychologie* helps illuminate this binaristic orientation. He asserts that identification is "the earliest expression of an emotional tie with another person."[28] In the usual course of events, the little boy "takes his father as his ideal", and, together with the "straightforward sexual object-cathexis towards hist mother", the "normal Oedipus complex" is born.[29] This is a triadic configuration. The mass, however, is ultimately dyadic, insofar as the group – so closely bonded with one another as to be one entity – is cathected directly to the leader. In Freud's terms, as summarized by McAfee, all members "internaliz[e] the leader as an ego ideal, finding commonality with others who have also internalized the same ego ideal"[30]. To protect the newly important group identity, people come to thoroughly demonize those who are different from themselves and the idealizing relationship to the father-leader is shorn of the ambivalence of the oedipal identification, in which "tenderness" toward and "wish for [...] removal" of the father are equally present.[31]

In the terms of my argument, the Thirdness that Freud takes for granted in the paradigmatic groups he describes early in his essay disappears in the process of a "regression of mental activity to an earlier stage such as we are not surprised to find among savages or children."[32] We are here in the presence of the *Urhorde*, which Freud designates as the primal state of both individual and group psychology, where the abstraction of equal fatherly *love* for each member of the group is replaced by a visceral collective *fear*. In the horde, "all of the sons knew that they were equally *persecuted* by the primal father, and *feared* him equally."[33] Returning to today, what we see in the relationship of disenfranchised men to powerful masculine figures seems to be idealization, not fear. But the absoluteness of the idealization masks an equally absolute negative obverse. Structurally speaking there is a doubling of dichotomies. Alongside the rampant splitting along the lines of projective identification – the mass splits off that within itself that it hates or fears and assigns it to a subhuman scapegoat who is then perceived to represent a potentially fatal threat to the group – there is splitting within the relationship to the powerful. For every beloved Trump there must be a hated and feared "elite" – à la Dr. Fauci – whose agenda is to eliminate the group's identity altogether.

Even a cursory glance at the media reveals a nearly infinite proliferation of dangers that America and the West supposedly must ward off. Race- and religion based identities form the greatest threat, according to the right wing; the "great replacement" conspiracy theory imagines migrants from the Global South, as well as Black and brown people in general, eclipsing the white culture of the Global North that has heretofore dominated the world. But gender is at least as prominent a battlefield as migration. If "our" jobs and benefits are at risk from the "flood" of migrants crossing our borders, "our" very continuation as a species is in danger from legal abortion, gay marriage, and trans people. In the face of progressive steps to acknowledge the fundamentally fluid nature of gender, conservatives scurry to (re)establish hard boundaries between male and female, masculine and feminine, just as they seek to build literal and figurative walls against migration. Their tools include not only the outright intimidation familiar from rallies that devolve into violent mobs,[34] but also manipulation of the legal system. In the plaintive cries of "reverse discrimination" against white men and the weaponization of the notion of "free speech" to protect racist, misogynistic, and homophobic demagoguery we witness how the abstractness of rationality can morph into the very opposite of what it is supposed to effect.

Here, too, the culprit is the collapsing of Thirdness into binarism. If at its inception Enlightenment Reason was imagined as facilitating the formation of subjects who could move about freely within the limits of a moral and epistemological framework that was taken to be universally valid, in our contemporary context reason is all too often reduced to a superficial collection of platitudes and false equivalencies. Martin Luther King's hope, for example, that his children would be "judged not by the color of their skin but by the content of their character" was, so to speak, a three-dimensional utterance, taking into account a complex history of race relations in the United States.[35] Today's so-called colorblindness flattens this rich dimensionality into a caricature of abstraction in which A is precisely equal to B, regardless of historical and experiential reality. White people, it says, can be equally victimized by discrimination as people of color. A similar reduction of complexity is visible in the arguments of gun advocates. Those who claim that the Second Amendment to the United States Constitution simply grants unfettered access to firearms refuse both the logical and the historical nuances of the Amendment.

The religious right represents an especially interesting case, since the invocation of secular principles to bolster religious claims reveals internal contradictions within the religious group itself. When a conservative graphic designer argues that the Constitutional guarantee of freedom of religion allows her to refuse service to gay customers, she not only pits anti-discrimination laws against her – and, alas, the conservative Supreme Court's – reading of the First Amendment, she also enacts a profound tension inside her own belief system. Rudden has described this phenomenon well: "Their group ego ideal is split, on the one hand condemning the Other while on the other claiming to embrace all as their Christ urged them to do."[36] She goes on to note the effect of this internal contradiction: "Here one can witness the adoption of a psychotic mode of defense within a group whose members are not necessarily individually psychotic."[37] Paranoid-schizoid splitting between the ostensibly pure and righteous self and the contaminating other shrouds the *internal* discord underlying such behaviors as excluding queer people from Christian churches. In the denial of their own internal conflicts, the group becomes a pure victim, mobilizing an identity narrative based in unique grievance and victimization: my group has suffered beyond all others at the hand of the ruthless powers that have swept aside my essential self, it says.

The absence of the Third can also help explain the profoundly contradictory relationship to authority in contemporary ultra-conservative movements: the same figures who worship the strong man reject, often violently, the authority of the government. The phenomenon presents itself most starkly in the close correlation between right-wing extremism and the military, the other father-centered group cited by Freud. Investigations into the January 6 riot have determined that four out of the five Proud Boys militiamen indicted on sedition charges had connections to the military; three of those charged are currently serving. One expert on domestic terrorism has declared that right-wing extremism in the military "is the single biggest threat to the security of the country."[38] In one recently revealed case, a young National Guardsman "kept a framed photo of Adolf Hitler by his bed and wanted to 'mag dump a crowd of Black Lives Matter protesters, especially the darker ones.'" In another, a soldier planned "to physically remove as many [Black and brown people] [...] by whatever means need be." Lest we think that the wrath of these young men is directed only toward what they regard as external threats to the country they "serve," jokes about "government collapse, authoritarian rule, and civil war"[39] abound on the "Degeneracy" group chat. Indeed, "government collapse" is already stealthily present: the servicemen described here were all *honorably* discharged by the military. It is worth noting that in the context of the all-volunteer military, many soldiers belong to the "millions of men [who] lack access to [the] kind of power and success"[40] embodied by the still-male elite. Paradoxically, in the *absence* of a structural Third, the men feel betrayed by the "system"; instead, they admire – even idolize – powerful figures who are winners in the neoliberal race to the top. Sheer power has replaced the authorizing Third; in its presence, one has two possible courses of action –hypothetically, at least: submit to it or grab it for yourself. These two apparently opposite "options" reveal themselves to be two sides of the same phenomenon as we are experiencing it today in the right-wing mass.

The complex relationship of this mass in both its Christian nationalist and militaristic dimensions to its enemies and its heroes alike is analyzed by Noëlle McAfee, invoking Fanon, in terms of *phobia* and *fetish* as means of skirting the oedipal "no". When the negative affect of fear is displaced onto a self-created phobic object "endowed with outsized malevolent power", the phobic subject is able to enjoy secretly, unconsciously, the "racist fantasy that civilization is white and blackness is accursed"[41] – or, I would add, the fantasy that sex is irrevocably binary and the male is absolutely superior. In this way, the anxiety associated with internal contradiction is assuaged by making a clean conscious distinction that allows both "justifiable" fear and unconscious enjoyment of that which is societally prohibited. Specifically, I consciously and publicly adhere to the legal or religious expectation of equal treatment for all while indulging my unconscious bias against the other, a bias that is in turn implicitly sanctioned by systems that turn a blind eye to racial profiling or even enshrine it in policy.[42] The leader-figure, in turn, becomes a fetish, which allows fantasized fulfillment of desires prohibited by the oedipal paternal function – indeed, it is the father himself who becomes the fetishistic object in this case. As Donald Trump famously joked during a campaign stop at a Christian college, "I could stand in the middle of Fifth Avenue and shoot somebody, and I wouldn't lose any voters."

It is important to note the temporal dimension of splitting. Freud, borrowing from Wilfred Trotter, emphasized the regressive quality of the herd instinct, which "turns away from anything that is new or unusual. The herd instinct would appear to be something primary, something which cannot be split up."[43] Similarly, in right-wing masses tradition becomes sacred as the arbiter of an identity that must not be changed at any cost, and nostalgia is the currency with which group identity is assured – more precisely, *nostos*, as explained by Svetlana Boym: "*Algia* (or longing) is what we share, yet *nostos* (or the return home) is what divides us. The promise to rebuild the ideal home lies at the core of many powerful ideologies today, tempting us to relinquish critical thinking for emotional bonding"[44]. Conservative groups are organized around the loss of an idealized past – often a "phantom homeland, for the sake of which one is ready to die or kill"[45]. If the core identity of the Make America

Great *Again* movement is based in a lost imaginary past, its continuation is projected into the future in the form of a powerful knight in shining armor who can remedy the harm that has been done to me. This figure embodies the imagined omnipotence that has been lost. In the words of pastor Peters: "We consider the left in our nation today to be a giant bully [...]. And when there is a bully on the schoolyard and somebody rises up and punches back, 'Hallelujah!' So we are thankful for Trump"[46]. On the most straightforward level, the leader figure is generated by these religiously inflected groups as an ally, even a savior as they "indulge in fantasies of rescue from anxieties"[47].

The appeal of the right-wing savior figure lies in a double illusion: he is simultaneously the *perfect* icon of the absolute power to which I aspire and *exactly* like me. His objective status as member of the very financial elite that has disempowered the working class is elided; instead, he at once descends to the level of "ordinary guy" and ascends to classless magnificence. For the Christian nationalists, a Trump rally is "a safe place, a Church where the like-minded can join together in a sea of red hats, [...] reveling in the ecstasy of knowing what a great man knows."[48] *Ecstasy* – this goes beyond idealization, even beyond the notion of introjection that Freud borrowed from Ferenczi[49] to a kind of fusion: in the mass, the group "focuse[s] fully on their leader to a degree to which they not only identify with him or her, as is a normal aspect of group life, but seem to absorb him as an intrinsic, urgent, and necessary part of themselves and of their identity"[50]. Ultimately, the crumbling of trust in a shared and self-evident legitimacy (whether it be associated with science, the government, or other institutions) – the triadic structure taken for granted by Freud – has devolved into an apocalyptic fear of + yearning for collapse. This catastrophe can, so the fantasy goes, only be prevented by an absolute/absolutistic savior who – paradoxically – simultaneously enacts the system's disintegration. In other words, the absolut(istic) dyad tends toward a merger – a oneness – that is longed for, but also, and ultimately, dangerous.

Especially in a patriarchal context, pining for a lost originary unity with a maternally-oriented "home" is a prominent trope, whether it takes the form of a beloved who understands me perfectly without language or a political movement that idealizes – and in cases like Putin's Russia, weaponizes – a "motherland" that has been unfairly destroyed by outside forces. But if the only perceived safe state is absolute fusion, which brings with it absolute omnipotence, this yearning is necessarily paired with profound anxiety. In analyzing "the search for an omnipotent leader with whom to establish a kind of fused or magical connection", Rudden, building on the Bionian Earl Hopper, associates attempts at fusion ("massification") with "a high degree of annihilation anxiety, that is, a fear of internal fragmentation"[51]. This kind of anxiety goes beyond that associated with unrecognized internal contradictions – or rather it lies *behind* or *before* those other anxieties. For a fear of identity loss can be unconsciously based in a deeper fear that is associated with an earlier stage of development.

The anxiety of the right-wing mass in the face of the phobic objects it has constructed for itself is secondary to fear of fundamental abandonment generated by the market ideology that pits everyone against everyone in a ruthless scramble for existence. Freud already noted that panic emerges in the group when it experiences a loss of faith in ("Irrewerden an") the paternal leader-figure, but the absence of the maternal function at the most primal level, which Winnicott terms the "holding environment," generates an even more profound terror. By "maternal function" I understand that which guarantees what Winnicott calls "a simple and stable going on being"[52]. Its absence generates a drastic threat: "Being and annihilation are the two alternatives. The holding environment therefore has as its main function the reduction to a minimum of impingements to which the infant must react with resultant annihilation of personal being"[53]. "Impingements" are disruptions (or "interruptions," in Winnicott's term) of the most basic human functions. In the political context we are dealing with here, such interruptions could involve the hunger that comes with food insecurity or being too cold or too hot when one can't afford heat or air conditioning. Psychically, perpetual worry about becoming ill in the absence of health insurance and the precarity of the gig economy interrupts being and threatens annihilation. Hence behind the paternal focus that drives Freud's argument –and behind the mostly masculine MAGA movement – lies a maternal function whose invisibility in both contexts belies its crucial importance.

A complex dynamic that differs subtly from Freud's model thus inheres in the MAGA movement. Freud could take for granted a structural Third that undergirds his exemplary groups, the church and the military. In this context, masses based on hypnotic suggestibility represent regression to a fundamentally dyadic relationship to the paternal function where power replaces legitimacy and universal fear of the father replaces his self-evident love for all. In our current situation, an even more existential fear is fueled not only by the absence of the Third but also by a systematic dismantling of a social infrastructure that guarantees provision of the most essential care, something we generally associate with the maternal function, regardless of precisely who or what is providing it. In response arises the fantasy of a clear dichotomy in which a perfectly pure self is threatened by an absolutely evil other that wants to penetrate the self's boundaries and plunge it into annihilation. The only defense against this disaster, according to the fantasy, is a figure who is simultaneously just like me and infinitely more powerful than me. As one old-style conservative commentator put it, astounded at the continued passionate support for Donald Trump despite criminal indictments, corruption revelations, and an objective threat to national security, for his disciples, "the former president is the only candidate to be trusted, the exclusive remedy to our corrupt system, the lone meaningful defender of God, flag and country. Debate is futile"[54]. His astonishment joins that of liberals who continue to decry right-wing extremists as deviants from a norm framed by universally-valid principles, ignoring the structural changes that have reduced authority to naked power and truth-seeking to fantasy-mongering.

Notes

[1] S. Freud, *Group Psychology and the Analysis of the Ego* (1921), *SE* 18, pp. 65-116, p. 69 (emphasis in the original).
[2] S. Freud, *Group Psychology*, p. 88.
[3] Ibid., p. 90.
[4] See ibid., p. 93.
[5] Ibid., p. 94.
[6] J. P. Muller, 'A View from Riggs: Treatment Resistance and Patient Authority-IV: Why the Pair Needs the Third', in: *Journal of the American Academy of Psychoanalysis* 35/2 (2007), pp. 221-241, p. 227.
[7] Ibid., p. 231 (emphasis in the original).
[8] J. Lacan, 'Seminar on "The Purloined Letter" (1956)', in: *The Purloined Poe*, J. Muller & W. Richardson (Eds.). Baltimore, MD: Johns Hopkins University Press, 1987, pp. 28-54, p. 35.
[9] J. Lacan, *Écrits: A Selection*, B. Fink (Transl.). New York: Norton, 2004, p. 164 and 293 respectively, quoted in J. P. Muller, 'A View from Riggs', p. 227.
[10] In Britton's terms: "The closure of the oedipal triangle by the recognition of the link joining the parents provides a limiting boundary for the internal world. It creates what I call a 'triangular space,' i.e., a space bounded by the three persons of the oedipal situation and all their potential relationships." R. Britton, 'Subjectivity, Objectivity, and Triangular Space', in: *Psychoanalytic Quarterly* 73 (2004), pp. 47-61, p. 47.
[11] J. P. Muller, 'A View from Riggs', p. 234.
[12] S. Freud, *Group Psychology*, p. 96 (emphasis mine).
[13] Ibid., p. 97.
[14] J. P. Muller, 'A View from Riggs', p. 234.

[15] See my *The Creative Self: Beyond Individualism*, co-authored with Mari Ruti. My discussion of neoliberalism owes a great deal to the clear, concise outline of its history by George Monbiot in *The Guardian* that appeared – presciently – six months before the election of Donald Trump in 2016 https://www.theguardian.com/books/2016/apr/15/neoliberalism-ideology-problem-george-monbiot (accessed 02-07-2023).

[16] J. Gentile, 'Close But No Cigar: The Perversion of Agency and the Absence of Thirdness', in: *Contemporary Psychoanalysis* 34/4 (2001), pp. 623-654, p. 629.

[17] D. Marriott, *Whither Fanon: Studies in the Blackness of Being*. Stanford, CA: Stanford University Press, 2018, cited in: N. McAfee, 'Racists, Fascists, and Other Dejects: Authoritarianism Reconsidered', p. 27 (unpublished manuscript).

[18] J. Gentile, 'Close But No Cigar', p. 640.

[19] See Emba: "Worrying about the state of our men is an American tradition. But today's problems are real and well documented. Deindustrialization, automation, free trade and peacetime have shifted the labor market dramatically, and not in men's favor – the need for physical labor has declined, while soft skills and academic credentials are increasingly rewarded. Growing numbers of working-age men have detached from the labor market, with the biggest drop in employment among men ages 25 to 34. For those in a job, wages have stagnated everywhere except the top." C. Emba, 'Men are lost. Here's a map out of the wilderness', in: *Washington Post*, July 10, 2023. https://www.washingtonpost.com/opinions/2023/07/10/christine-emba-masculinity-new-model/?utm_campaign=wp_post_most&utm_medium=email&utm_source=newsletter&wpisrc=nl_most (accessed 02-07-2023).

[20] J. Gentile, 'Close But No Cigar', p. 633.

[21] J. Lacan, 'The Mirror Stage as Formative of the Function of the I as Revealed in Psychoanalytic Experience (1949)', in: *Écrits*, A. Sheridan (Transl.). New York: Norton, 1977, p. 1-7, p. 2.

[22] J. Burnett, 'Christian nationalism is still thriving – and is a force for returning Trump to Power', in: *National Public Radio*, January 23, 2022. https://www.npr.org/2022/01/14/1073215412/christian-nationalism-donald-trump (accessed 02-07-2023).

[23] M. Orozco-Guzmán, H. Soria-Escalante & J. Quiroz-Bautista, 'Narcissistic Isomorphisms: The Ego, the Masses, the Urvater, and the Alterity', in: *Psychotherapy and Politics International* 19 (2021/3), pp. 1-11, p. 1.

[24] A. Bass, 'The Problem of "Concreteness"', in: *Psychoanalytic Quarterly* 66 (1997), pp. 642-682, p. 671.

[25] J. P. Muller, 'A View from Riggs', p. 236. Britton notes that triangularity "provides us with a capacity for entertaining another point of view whilst retaining our own, for reflecting on ourselves whilst being ourselves" (R. Britton, 'Subjectivity, Objectivity, and Triangular Space, pp. 47-38, p. 47 f.

[26] J. P. Muller, 'A View from Riggs', p. 235-236.

[27] CNN, 'Facts First', https://edition.cnn.com/factsfirst/politics/factcheck_c791ae08-1e5b-4458-a3a8-6c8449e1bc9f (accessed 02-07-2023).

[28] S. Freud, *Group Psychology*, p. 105.

[29] Ibid.

[30] N. McAfee, 'Racists, Fascists, and Other Dejects', p. 5.

[31] S. Freud, *Group Psychology*, p. 105.

[32] Ibid., p. 117. Freud explicitly juxtaposes here the "common groups" to the "highly organized groups" he has already discussed.

[33] Ibid., p. 125.

[34] As in the "Unite the Right" rally in Charlottesville, Virginia on August 12, 2017, in which "Neo-Nazis, Ku Klux Klansmen and other white supremacists marched through the University of Virginia campus bearing torches and terrorizing students with chants of 'Blood and soil' and 'Jews will not replace us'". On the second day of the rally, "Neo-Nazi James Fields rammed his car into the crowd, injuring dozens of people and killing 32-year-old Heather Heyer" (D. Elliott, 'The Charlottesville rally 5 years later: "It's what you're still trying to forget"', in: *National Public Radio*, August 12, 2022. https://www.npr.org/2022/08/12/1116942725/the-charlottes-ville-rally-5-years-later-its-what-youre-still-trying-to-forget (accessed 02-07-2023).

[35] J. Washington, Jesse. 'Martin Luther King Jr. "content of character" quote inspires debate', in: *Associated Press/MassLive*, January 21, 2013. https://www.masslive.com/news/2013/01/martin_luther_king_jr_content.html (accessed 02-07-2023).

[36] M. G. Rudden, 'Insurrection in the U.S. Capitol: Understanding Psychotic, Projective, and Introjective Group Processes', in: *International Journal of Applied Psychoanalytic Studies* 18/4 (2021), pp. 372-384, p. 375.

[37] Ibid., p. 375 f.

[38] H. Krueger, '"The single biggest threat to the security of the country": Extremism in the military is alarming experts', in: *Boston Globe*, July 16, 2023. https://www.bostonglobe.com/2023/07/15/nation/extremism-in-military-big-security-threat/?s_campaign=breakingnews:newsletter (accessed 02-07-2023).

[39] Ibid.

[40] C. Emba, 'Men are lost'.

[41] N. McAfee, 'Racists, Fascists, and Other Dejects', p. 8.

[42] See for example the so-called "Stand Your Ground Laws", which render legal the harming, or even killing, of someone perceived to be a threat to one's person or one's property – almost exclusively people of color – while allowing the aggressor – almost exclusively white people – to continue to claim that they are not racist. See https://en.wikipedia.org/wiki/Stand-your-ground_law (accessed 02-07-2023).

[43] S. Freud, *Group Psychology*, p. 118.

[44] S. Boym, 'Nostalgia and its Discontents', in: *The Hedgehog Review* (Summer 2007), pp. 1-18, p. 9.

[45] Ibid., p. 10.

[46] J. Burnett, 'Christian nationalism is still thriving'.

[47] M. G. Rudden, 'Insurrection in the U.S. Capitol', p. 375.

[48] J. Sharlet, 'The Second Coming', in: *Vanity Fair*, July/August 2020. https://archive.vanityfair.com/article/2020/7/the-second-coming (accessed 02-07-2023).

[49] See S. Freud, *Group Psychology*, p. 113 and 127.

[50] M. G. Rudden, 'Insurrection in the U.S. Capitol', p. 373.

51 Ibid., p. 376.
52 D. W. Winnicott, 'The Theory of the Parent-Infant Relationship', in: *International Journal of Psycho-Analysis* 41 (1960), pp. 585-595, p. 587.
53 Ibid., p. 591.
54 G. Abernathy, 'I thought the GOP would abandon Trump. I was wrong', in: *The Washington Post*, July 17, 2023. https://www.washingtonpost.com/opinions/2023/07/17/donald-trump-gop-voters-2024-race/?utm_campaign=wp_post_most&utm_medium=email&utm_source=newsletter&wpisrc=nl_most (accessed 02-07-2023).

Ricardo Ainslie holds the M.K. Hage Centennial Professorship in Education at the University of Texas at Austin in the Department of Educational Psychology and serves as director of research and education for AMPATH Mexico at Dell Medical School. In addition to publishing regularly in academic journals, his books include *The Fight to Save Juárez: Life in the Heart of Mexico's Drug War* (University of Texas Press, 2013), and *Long Dark Road: The story of Bill King and Murder in Jasper, Texas* (University of Texas Press, 2004). In 2022, he was the Fulbright-Freud Visiting Scholar at the Sigmund Freud Museum in Vienna. He is currently working on *City and Psyche*, a book about cities and communities as psychological spaces.

Giuseppina Antinucci is a Fellow of the British Psychoanalytic Society (BPS) and full Member of the International Psychoanalytical Association (*IPA*). She trained and worked in London for many years, in private practice and institutional settings. She presently lives in Milan, where she works with adults. She also works remotely with patients and teaches and supervises in Britain, China, and the US. She is on the Editorial Boards of the *International Journal of Psychoanalysis* and *Psychoanalytic Quarterly*. She has published several papers on the IJP and has contributed chapters in books, among which *When the body speaks* (Routledge, 2021) and *Psychoanalysis, Identity, and Internet* (Karnac, 2016). Giuseppina Antinucci has a special interest in the intersection of psychoanalysis and the arts. She is writing a monograph on this subject, titled "Psychoanalytic engagement with the arts. Kultur and culture" which will be published by Routledge.

Helmut Dahmer, professor emeritus, studied sociology and philosophy with Helmuth Plessner, Theodor W. Adorno and Jürgen Habermas. From 1968 to 1992 he edited the psychoanalytical monthly *Psyche*. In 1984 he was on the founding advisory board of the Hamburg Institute for Social Research. From 1974 to 2002 he taught sociology at the Technical University of Darmstadt. Guest professorships have taken him to Berne, Innsbruck and Lima. He is editing a selected edition of Trotsky's writings, calculated to comprise 12 volumes. Publications *Libido und Gesellschaft* (1973, 1982, expanded new edition 2013); *Pseudonatur und Kritik* (1994; 2013); *Soziologie nach einem barbarischen Jahrhundert* (2001); *Die unnatürliche Wissenschaft* (2012, 2019); *Freud, Trotzki und der Horkheimer-Kreis* (2019, second edition 2020); *Antisemitismus, Xenophobie, Amnesie* (2020); *Trotzki, die Psychoanalyse und die kannibalischen Regime* (2022).

Jan De Vos holds an MA in psychology and a PhD in philosophy. Currently he is affiliated to University College Ghent (Belgium). His main interests are the critique of (neuro)psychology, (neuro)psychologisation, and, related to this, the subject of the digital turn. His inspiration is continental philosophy, Freudo-Lacanian theory and ideology critique. His books include *The Digitalisation of (Inter)Subjectivity A Psy-critique of the Digital Death Drive* (2020), *The Metamorphoses of the Brain. Neurologisation and its Discontents* (2016) and *Psychologisation in Times of Globalisation* (2012). http://janrdevos. weebly.com

Daniela Finzi is a literary and cultural scholar. She is member of the board of the Sigmund Freud Foundation and, as head of the research department of the Sigmund Freud Museum, is in charge of the academic exhibitions, research projects and conference program of Berggasse 19. She is also a board member of "aka – Arbeitskreis Kulturanalyse" and co-editor of the book series *aka\texte and Sigmund Freuds Werke. Wiener Interdisziplinäre Kommentare*. She has written on cultural theor & psychoanalysis, gender studies and Balkan studies.

Francisco J. González, MD, is Personal & Supervising Analyst, Community Psychoanalysis Supervising Analyst, and Faculty at the Psychoanalytic Institute of Northern California (PINC), where he also helped found and serves as Co-Director of the Community Psychoanalysis Track. He is on the faculty of the NYU Postdoctoral Program in Psychoanalysis and a Supervising Analyst at the Massachusetts Institute for Psychoanalysis. He serves on the editorial boards of *Psychoanalytic Dialogues*, *JAPA*, and *Parapraxis* and on the Holmes Commission on Racial Equality in American Psychoanalysis. He practices privately in San Francisco and Oakland and in the public domain at Instituto Familiar de la Raza in San Francisco.

Earl Hopper, PhD, is a psychoanalyst, group analyst, certified group therapist, and organizational consultant in private practice in London. A Distinguished Fellow of the American Group Psychotherapy Association, an Honorary Member of the Group Analytic Society International, and an Honorary Member of the Institute of Group Analysis, he is a supervisor and training analyst for many psychotherapy organizations in England. He is also a former President of the International Association for Group Psychotherapy and Group Processes (IAGP), and a former Chairman of the Association of Independent Psychoanalysts of the British Psychoanalytical Society. Hopper has published and edited many books and articles in psychoanalysis, group analysis and sociology, he is the editor of *The New International Library of Group Analysis (NILGA)* for Routledge.

Ranjana Khanna is Director of the John Hope Franklin Humanites Institute and Professor of English, GSF, and the Literature Program at Duke University. She works on Anglo- and Francophone Postcolonial theory and literature, and Film, Psychoanalysis, and Feminist theory. She has published widely on transnational feminism, psychoanalysis, and postcolonial and feminist theory, literature, and film. She is the author of *Dark Continents: Psychoanalysis and Colonialism* (Duke University Press, 2003) and *Algeria Cuts: Women and Representation 1830 to the present* (Stanford University Press, 2008.) She has published in journals like *Differences, Signs, Third Text, Diacritics, Screen, Art History, positions, SAQ, Feminist Theory,* and *Public Culture*. Her current book manuscripts in progress are called: *Asylum: The Concept and the Practice* and *Technologies of Unbelonging*.

Sama Maani, born in Graz, grew up in Austria, Germany and Iran. Studied medicine in Vienna and philosophy in Zurich. Trained as a psychiatrist and psychoanalyst. Today lives as a writer in Vienna. Publications include: *Ungläubig* (novel, 2014), *Respektverweigerung: Warum wir fremde Kulturen nicht respektieren sollten. Und die eigene auch nicht* (essay volume, 2015), *Der Heiligenscheinorgasmus und andere Erzählungen* (2016), *Teheran Wunderland* (novel, 2018), *Warum wir Linke über den Islam nicht reden können* (essay volume, 2019); *Zizek in Teheran* (novel, 2021); *Warum ich über den Islam nicht mehr rede. Schwierige Meinungen über Politik, Kunst, Literatur und Geschichte* (essay volume, 2022) and in 2023 the essay volume *Warum uns der Iran nicht wurscht sein sollte. Und Sigmund Freud und Robert Musil auch nicht.*

Ulrike May, studies in psychology and psychoanalytic training in Munich (DPV, IPA). 1980 to 1998 practice in Munich, 1999 to 2020 practice in Berlin. Teaching and supervision. Numerous publications on the history of psychoanalytic theory and on Freud's practice based on his hitherto unknown patient diaries; see bibliography at www.may-schroeter.de. Most recently, among other things, together with Michael Schröter: new edition of Freud's *Jenseits des Lustprinzips* with a first publication of the preliminary version of this text from 1919 (May & Schröter 2013), anthology of own publications: *Freud bei der Arbeit* (Psychosozial-Verlag 2015), and *Der Abschied vom Primat des Sexuellen. Zur Geschichte der Psychoanalyse in Berlin und London zwischen 1920 und 1925* (Psychosozial-Verlag 2023).

Gail Newman is the Harold J Henry Professor of German and Comparative Literature at Williams College in Williamstown, Massachusetts USA. Her research centers on questions of subjectivity in the context of narrative and language, especially as they relate to trauma and incomprehensibility. Her work is informed by an eclectic mix of psychoanalytic theories, including Freud's, Lacan's, Ferenczi's, and Winnicott's. Her most recent publication is co-authored with Mari Ruti, and will come out in January 2025: *The Creative Self: Beyond Individualism* (Columbia University Press).

Jeanne Wolff Bernstein, Ph.D. works as a psychoanalyst in Vienna. She was president and training analyst at the Psychoanalytic Institute of Northern California (PINC) in San Francisco. She teaches at The New York University Postdoctoral Program of Psychoanalysis and Psychotherapy in New York. She is a member of the Wiener Arbeitskreis für Psychoanalyse. Jeanne Wolff Bernstein is the chair of the advisory board of the Sigmund Freud Foundation in Vienna, and was the 2008 Fulbright-Freud Visiting Lecturer of Psychoanalysis at the Sigmund Freud Museum, Vienna. She has written extensively on psychoanalysis and the visual arts and on the work of Jacques Lacan.

www.ingramcontent.com/pod-product-compliance
Lightning Source LLC
Chambersburg PA
CBHW050608280326
41932CB00016B/2961